Around the Word
in 60 Seconds

Happy 12th Birthday!

Hope you enjoy this Book

Love,
Matt, Cindy
& Kids

MARY DeMUTH

in partnership with iShine Ministries

AROUND the WORD
in 60 SECONDS
the ultimate tween devotional

TYNDALE™
MOMENTUM

An Imprint of
Tyndale House Publishers, Inc.

Visit Tyndale online at www.tyndale.com.

Visit Tyndale Momentum online at www.tyndalemomentum.com.

TYNDALE is a registered trademark of Tyndale House Publishers, Inc. *Tyndale Momentum* and the Tyndale Momentum logo are trademarks of Tyndale House Publishers, Inc. Tyndale Momentum is an imprint of Tyndale House Publishers, Inc.

Around the Word in 60 Seconds: The Ultimate Tween Devotional

Designed by Jacqueline L. Nuñez and Beth Sparkman

Edited by Bonne Steffen

Published in association with the literary agency of Esther Fedorkevich, Fedd and Company, Inc., 606 Flamingo Blvd., Austin, TX 78734.

Scripture quotations are taken from the *Holy Bible*, New Living Translation, copyright © 1996, 2004, 2007 by Tyndale House Foundation. Used by permission of Tyndale House Publishers, Inc., Carol Stream, Illinois 60188. All rights reserved.

For manufacturing information regarding this product, please call 1-800-323-9400.

Library of Congress Cataloging-in-Publication Data

DeMuth, Mary E., date.
  Around the Word in 60 seconds : the ultimate tween devotional / Mary DeMuth in partnership with iShine Ministries.
    p. cm.
  ISBN 978-1-4143-6392-9 (sc)
  1. Preteens—Religious life—Juvenile literature. I. Title.
  BV4870.D46 2012
  242'.62—dc23   2012015825

Printed in the United States of America

18   17   16   15   14   13   12
7   6   5   4   3   2   1

Contents

Acknowledgments

To my family who endured a summer month with me typing, thank you.

Thanks to the conscientious and bright staff at Tyndale, and the hearts of the folks at iShine. You made this an impactful book.

Thanks to Esther, my agent and friend, who shepherded this project.

Hugs to my prayer team for praying me through this book: Twilla Fontenot, Ashley Weis, Kevin and Renee Bailey, Carla Smith, Caroline Coleman, Cheramy Mayfield, Colleen Eslinger, Jeanne Damoff, Darren and Holly Sapp, D'Ann Mateer, Dorian Coover-Cox, Erin Teske, Katy Gedney, Kimberly Baker, Ginger Vassar, Helen Graves, Holly Schmidt, Jan Winebrenner, Jen Powell, Kathy ONeall, Katy Raymond, Denise Willhite, Anita Curtis, Diane Klapper, Lesley Hamilton, Leslie Wilson, Lilli Brenchley, Liz Wolf, Marcia Robbins, Marcus Goodyear, Grace Bower, Marybeth Whalen, Pam LeTourneau, Paula Moldenhauer, Rae McIlrath, Phyllis Yount, Becky Ochs, Sandi Glahn, Sarah Walker, Shawna Marie Bryant, Tim Riter, Tina Howard,

Tracy Walker, Heidi VanDyken, Paul Napari, Renee Mills, Stacey Tomisser, John Davis, Carla Williams, Nicole Baart, Tosca Lee, Marilyn Scholtz, TJ Wilson, Jim Rubart, Patrick DeMuth, Jody Capehart, Susan Meissner, Ariel Lawhon, Mary Vestal, Amy Sorrells, Lisa Shea, Dena Dyer, Kathryn Thomas, Carol Avery, Cyndi Kraweitz, Don Pape, Esther Fedorkevich, Susie Larson, Christy Tennant, Jodi Vinson, and Ericka Smiley.

To the DeMuth advisory board, thank you for your wisdom, listening ear, and sage advice: Randy Ingermanson, Jody Capehart, Holly Schmidt, Cathleen Lewis, Kimberly Baker, Stacey Tomisser, Denise Martin, Patrick DeMuth, Pam LeTourneau, Heidi VanDyken, Alice Crider, Leslie Wilson, and D'Ann Mateer.

Jesus, thanks for being the reason I write.

Introduction

ARE YOU READY for your life to be changed? I can't guarantee the words in this devotional have superpowers, but I do know this: Jesus is in the business of radically changing lives. Getting to know Him is an adventure, and this book is a road map for that adventure. Think of it as your daily journey with Jesus over the next fifty-two weeks.

Here's how to use the map. Every week, read the first entry. Usually this will be on a Monday as you start your school week (or summer week!). On that day you'll be given an activity to accomplish during that seven-day period. This will take more than sixty seconds, but it will be well worth your time. You'll also find a prayer you can use that day to get you started, but please stay connected to Jesus throughout the week!

The sixty-second commitment comes during the rest of the week. You'll have five verses to read and respond to, four for the rest of the week, and a fifth for the weekend. How you respond to the verses is up to you. Of course, you can write out your answer to the question following the verse, but you may want to be more original—sketch something, write a prayer or a poem, make a collage, or take a photo and paste it in the space provided. Use whatever creative process inspires you the most. You might find your one-minute time slot stretching longer because you're having so much fun interacting with the verses.

While the stories in this book are fictional, many of the details are adapted from my life and the lives of the kids I disciple. In that sense, they are real. You might even see yourself in the situations described. I firmly believe that you can better understand the Bible when a story is wrapped around it. That's why Jesus told so many stories, and it's why when we hear a sermon at church, we often remember the stories the longest.

Remember, you bring yourself to this book. How you grow and change and come closer to Jesus depends on your willingness to let the verses and stories and prayers sink deep into your heart. Being a Jesus-follower isn't about doing a bunch of good things so others will think you're a Christian. It's not about playacting and pretending. It's about your heart.

Great things flow from a changed, renewed heart. And Jesus loves-loves-loves to scrub you clean, set you free, and get you on your feet beside Him.

I'm so excited you're taking this personal journey. I'm thrilled that your life with Jesus may be completely changed and renewed because of it. I'm excited not only about what could happen to you, but also about all the lives you will touch because of your spiritual growth.

As the journey begins, would you pray with me right now?

Dear Jesus, I want my heart changed from the inside out. I want this book to change me. Help me to see it as a road map toward the adventure of knowing You. Use the stories to teach me. I pray that the verses will change me. And may the prayers be true to me and my relationship with You. Help me to live for You. I love You and I trust You. Amen.

Mary DeMuth

★ DAY 1 —May 6th

"Build each other up in your most holy faith, pray in the power of the Holy Spirit, and await the mercy of our Lord Jesus Christ, who will bring you eternal life. In this way, you will keep yourselves safe in God's love."   Jude 1:20-21

FOR WEEKS BEFORE THE ELECTIONS, Tia boasted that she'd make a great eighth-grade class president and set out to prove it. During the campaign, every one of Tia's opponents gave speeches about the crowded hallways, the cafeteria food, and the need for vending machines. But Tia had a different approach. At an assembly for the candidates, she stood at the podium with two of the meanest boys in school on either side of her and yelled into the microphone, "Stand up!" Her two henchmen gestured wildly with their arms. One by one, everyone got to their feet. Tia shook her fist, then told the audience to clap. They did. Tia looked over the crowd. "Now that's power," she yelled. "If you want a powerful president, vote for me."

The class elected Tia, but she didn't make a great president. She wanted only the power and prestige of the office; she had no intention of serving the students. She complained and grumbled, but did nothing to fix any of the problems. She favored thugs and lost the respect of her classmates.

The Tias in the world—bullies who brag and get what they want by pretending to be your friend—are selfish and whiny. But as a follower of Jesus, you can choose to live differently. How? Read the second part of the Scripture passage above:

- *Build up others.* Take time to encourage a friend. Look beyond your own problems for the day and try to shoulder a friend's stress.
- *Pray in the power of the Holy Spirit.* How do you do that? Tell God your worries and fears. Ask Him to help you with the problems in your life and in the lives of your friends.
- *Await God's mercy.* Think about Jesus' act of extreme mercy when He gave His life on the cross. He died in your place. He left His position of power and majesty in heaven to come to this crazy earth and die for you and the Tias of this world. That's a big reason to thank Him!

Do you see what happens when you do all of these things? Jude concludes with these hopeful words: "In this way, you will keep yourselves safe in God's love." Sometimes we think being safe means acting like Tia—pushing people to do what we want, getting our own way so we're happy. But being safe is resting in God's love and letting Him be the powerful one.

✎ Take Action

Take a few minutes to think of someone in your life right now (friend, parent, brother, sister, relative) who could use some encouragement. Send that person a message via texting, Facebook, e-mail, or voice mail, or handwrite a note and drop it in the mail.

✝ Connect with Jesus

Jesus, I don't want to be like Tia, manipulating people to get my way or using power to hurt others. Help me encourage my hurting friends. Teach me to pray all day long so I feel close to You, even at school. And would You show me this week that You love me in a very specific me-shaped way? Thank You, Jesus. Amen.

Around the Word This Week

Each day this week, read a verse and respond to it however you want. Think about it. Write it down on an index card that you can carry with you. Journal about it. Share it with a friend. Pray that the verse will impact you and you will obey it. It's your choice. To get you started thinking about how the Scripture relates to your life, consider the question that follows it.

⭐ DAY 2 —May 7th

"Do everything without complaining and arguing, so that no one can criticize you. Live clean, innocent lives as children of God, shining like bright lights in a world full of crooked and perverse people."   Philippians 2:14-15

Who do you know who complains? Why do you think the person does that?

Parents because they don't feel appreciated.

⭐ DAY 3

"These people are grumblers and complainers, living only to satisfy their desires. They brag loudly about themselves, and they flatter others to get what they want." Jude 1:16

When was the last time you bragged about something to get attention?

Maybe about my xbox or zoo trip group.

 **DAY 4**

"Don't grumble about each other, brothers and sisters, or you will be judged. For look—the Judge is standing at the door!"

James 5:9

What is the silliest complaint about someone that you've ever made or heard someone else say?

They were singing too loud.

⭐ DAY 5

"Make allowance for each other's faults, and forgive anyone who offends you. Remember, the Lord forgave you, so you must forgive others. Above all, clothe yourselves with love, which binds us all together in perfect harmony. And let the peace that comes from Christ rule in your hearts. For as members of one body you are called to live in peace. And always be thankful."   Colossians 3:13-15

Who do you need to forgive right now? Why?

So you can move on with everything.

Over the Weekend

"You are my God, and I will praise you! You are my God, and I will exalt you! Give thanks to the LORD, for he is good! His faithful love endures forever." Psalm 118:28-29

How has God shown His faithful love to you this week?

Because I stayed safe on the Zoo trip.

WEEK TWO
Week

 DAY 1

"Remember, dear brothers and sisters, that few of you were wise in the world's eyes or powerful or wealthy when God called you. Instead, God chose things the world considers foolish in order to shame those who think they are wise. And he chose things that are powerless to shame those who are powerful. God chose things despised by the world, things counted as nothing at all, and used them to bring to nothing what the world considers important. As a result, no one can ever boast in the presence of God." 1 Corinthians 1:26-29

EVA LIVED A CHARMED LIFE IN JUNIOR HIGH. She was athletic, smart, popular, and funny. To celebrate graduating from eighth grade, she invited a small group of friends to go canoeing on the lake behind her home. They were so excited to celebrate that none of them put on life jackets, and they horsed around in the small canoe. It tilted back and forth while everyone laughed and splashed.

Everyone was enjoying the day until, suddenly, Alexia fell into the water. "I can't swim!" she cried out, struggling to stay afloat. Eva, who was an accomplished swimmer, dove in and tried to rescue Alexia, but Alexia pulled her under. Before emergency responders could get there, Alexia drowned. Eva survived, but she was permanently brain damaged.

You'd think Eva's life was over. Because of her limited ability to move due to the brain injury, the former athlete's muscles grew stiff. She couldn't form her thoughts clearly and her speech was slurred. Although initially her friends visited her in the rehab center, their visits eventually dropped off. And Eva's sense of humor faded. In her loneliness during recovery, she cried out to Jesus, asking Him to help her cope with what happened. He tenderly met her where she was and began to heal her heart.

Today if you met Eva, you'd feel like you had met with Jesus. Eva's simple praises with crooked hands raised to the heavens in worship inspire many to follow Jesus. She is a perfect example of God using someone who may look foolish to others to shame those who think they're all that.

Have you ever felt weak or foolish or overlooked or small or uncool? Take comfort in the fact that God chooses folks like Eva, like you, like all of us to shout about His strength and power. Some people feel they don't need Jesus' strength. Instead, they rely on their own abilities. But if you give your weakness to Jesus, He has a chance to really demonstrate His power through the very thing you think hinders you. That's terrific news. And that's why when God meets you where you are, you can boast in His abilities.

Like the apostle Paul explains in today's verse, God uses us no matter what. No matter how un-choose-able you feel, God has chosen you for a specific you-shaped reason. Thank Him for that today.

Take Action

God uses the foolish to shame the wise. In other words, He can use the weakest things about us to do great things and show His power. Be on the lookout this week for examples of that. Write a list of five times you saw God demonstrate His power through your weakness or the weakness of someone else.

Connect with Jesus

Jesus, thank You for choosing me, just me. Thanks that I don't have to be perfect for You to work through me. Thank You that when I feel weak, I can go to You and ask You to be strong. Open my eyes to see You working in my weakness this week, please. Amen.

Around the Word This Week

Each day this week, read a verse and respond to it however you want. Think about it. Write it down on an index card that you can carry with you. Journal about it. Share it with a friend. Pray that the verse will impact you and you will obey it. It's your choice. To get you started thinking about how the Scripture relates to your life, consider the question that follows it.

⭐ DAY 2

"I take pleasure in my weaknesses, and in the insults, hardships, persecutions, and troubles that I suffer for Christ. For when I am weak, then I am strong."

2 Corinthians 12:10

What do you think it means to take pleasure in your weakness? *To think of the happy/good sides of it.*

⭐ DAY 3

"I will give you all the proof you want that Christ speaks through me. Christ is not weak when he deals with you; he is powerful among you. Although he was crucified in weakness, he now lives by the power of God. We, too, are weak, just as Christ was, but when we deal with you we will be alive with him and will have God's power."   2 Corinthians 13:3-4

If you truly believed that God's power lived inside you, how would that change things for you this week?

I'd not care so much about what idiots say. I thought I already knew that though.

⭐ DAY 4

"And the Holy Spirit helps us in our weakness. For example, we don't know what God wants us to pray for. But the Holy Spirit prays for us with groanings that cannot be expressed in words." Romans 8:26

Have you ever been speechless before God? What happened? Why were you at a loss for words?

I don't think so yet. That isn't a bad thing though.

★ DAY 5

"If I must boast, I would rather boast about the things that show how weak I am. God, the Father of our Lord Jesus, who is worthy of eternal praise, knows I am not lying."

2 Corinthians 11:30-31

How, specifically, has God been strong in your weakness this week?

Over the Weekend

"Let us come boldly to the throne of our gracious God. There we will receive his mercy, and we will find grace to help us when we need it most." Hebrews 4:16

When was the last time you experienced God's kindness?

WEEK THREE
New

 ## DAY 1

"But forget all that—it is nothing compared to what I am going to do. For I am about to do something new. See, I have already begun! Do you not see it? I will make a pathway through the wilderness. I will create rivers in the dry wasteland."

Isaiah 43:18-19

SEVENTH GRADER SARAH was stuck in the past. Her mind kept going back to fourth grade, when her parents got a divorce. For weeks after her dad moved out, she'd spent a lot of time journaling about why it happened, wondering if there was something she could have done to stop it. She talked to her best friend, Avery, about it constantly. And she seldom smiled because, really, how could you smile when your family was broken up? In her mind, her life was a wilderness, a wasteland of empty promises.

Avery loved Sarah, but Sarah's sadness made her weary. She encouraged Sarah to talk to the school counselor because Avery didn't feel she could help Sarah anymore.

When Sarah met Mr. Johnson, she didn't think he looked or acted like a professional counselor with his long hair, casual clothes, and laid-back manner. But Mr. Johnson listened attentively to Sarah's story and asked lots of questions. Eventually he asked her something that startled her. "When is your life going to start again?"

"What do you mean?"

"Well, it seems like your life was hijacked three years ago and has been imprisoned ever since."

"I do want my life back," Sarah said quietly.

"I want you to start thinking differently," Mr. Johnson said. "All your worries about the past are making your life miserable right now. What would your life look like if you changed your focus from what happened in the past to what exciting thing might happen next?"

That question changed Sarah's perspective.

Isaiah, an Old Testament prophet, offers similar advice in today's Scripture. Often we spend so many hours, days, even weeks rehashing something painful that happened in the past that we forget about what God might do today. God can do the impossible. He can take the wilderness of our situation and make a pathway through the thorns and briar bushes. He graciously waters the dry wasteland of our pain with His love. Our job is simply to be aware, wait for Him, trust Him enough to stop looking back, and watch for what He will do in our lives.

✎ Take Action

Brainstorm! Dream up a way God could change a painful situation in your life. Write a prayer asking God to give you a different perspective on your situation.

✝ Connect with Jesus

Jesus, forgive me if I've chained myself to the past too much instead of seeing You working right now. Help me be aware of what You are doing in my life today and what You might do in my life tomorrow. I choose right now to give You my pain. Amen.

Around the Word This Week

Each day this week, read a verse and respond to it however you want. Think about it. Write it down on an index card that you can carry with you. Journal about it. Share it with a friend. Pray that the verse will impact you and you will obey it. It's your choice. To get you started thinking about how the Scripture relates to your life, consider the question that follows it.

DAY 2

"This means that anyone who belongs to Christ has become a new person. The old life is gone; a new life has begun!"

2 Corinthians 5:17

Who do you know who seems to have a new, joyful life?

⭐ DAY 3

"But that isn't what you learned about Christ. Since you have heard about Jesus and have learned the truth that comes from him, throw off your old sinful nature and your former way of life, which is corrupted by lust and deception. Instead, let the Spirit renew your thoughts and attitudes. Put on your new nature, created to be like God—truly righteous and holy."

Ephesians 4:20-24

What do you think it means to "put on your new nature"?

⭐ DAY 4

"By his death, Jesus opened a new and life-giving way through the curtain into the Most Holy Place. And since we have a great High Priest who rules over God's house, let us go right into the presence of God with sincere hearts fully trusting him. For our guilty consciences have been sprinkled with Christ's blood to make us clean, and our bodies have been washed with pure water."   Hebrews 10:20-22

Why is it so important that Jesus has washed us clean?

⭐ DAY 5

"Anyone with ears to hear must listen to the Spirit and understand what he is saying to the churches. To everyone who is victorious I will give some of the manna that has been hidden away in heaven. And I will give to each one a white stone, and on the stone will be engraved a new name that no one understands except the one who receives it."

Revelation 2:17

What would you like your new name to be? Healed? Joyful One? Beautiful? Strong?

Over the Weekend

"We died and were buried with Christ by baptism. And just as Christ was raised from the dead by the glorious power of the Father, now we also may live new lives."   Romans 6:4

Why is it important that Jesus was raised from the dead?

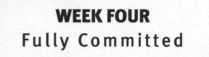

DAY 1

"The eyes of the LORD search the whole earth in order to strengthen those whose hearts are fully committed to him."

2 Chronicles 16:9

JED, A WIDE RECEIVER for his junior high team, loved football. He lived, breathed, ate, and worked out with it fully on his mind. He studied games he DVRed and read books about famous football players. He pored over the team playbook, memorizing each pattern. He practiced with his dad every day. Sometimes he stayed up past his bedtime, lying in bed and throwing a football toward the ceiling and catching it.

Jed was committed.

So when the coach needed a receiver in the last play of

the last game of the season, guess who he called on? "Jed," he said, "run the pattern just like we practiced last week." He placed his hands on Jed's shoulders and looked into his eyes. "You're ready for this. I have full confidence in you. Now go out there and catch that ball!"

Jed sprinted his pattern, doubled back, then waited in the end zone. The quarterback threw a perfect spiral. Jed leapt into the air, nabbed the ball, and fell to the ground, clutching the football like his life depended on it. Touchdown! Because Jed had practiced and prepared, he was ready for this moment.

God wants us to be like Jed when it comes to being dedicated to Him. Today's Scripture says God is looking everywhere—in every country, state, and town all over the world—for people who are fully committed to Him. He promises to support those who have abandoned themselves to the game He has planned for us on this earth.

How do we do that?

Study the playbook. If we want God's strength, we must understand His heart and what He desires. Reading the Bible isn't checking off verses on a list; it's a chance to get to know the greatest Coach in the universe. Approach it as a thrilling adventure instead of a boring "have to."

Practice. God sees that we are fully committed when we act on our beliefs. Have you noticed someone eating alone in the lunchroom? Head that direction and sit with that person.

Go out of your way to serve others, including your teachers. Your actions will make a big impact.

Watch others. Jed watched how NFL players handled game situations in order to learn from them. You can do the same thing by watching wiser, stronger Christians. By observing their behavior, you'll learn how to walk like Jesus.

✎ Take Action

Find someone to stalk (in a good way). Ask God to show you someone who "plays the game well" so you can learn too. Watch how that person treats others who are hurting. What surprises you about how the person lives his or her life? In what ways does the person show a full commitment to Jesus? How can you imitate your secret mentor?

✝ Connect with Jesus

Jesus, I realize Your eyes roam all over this earth looking for people who have fully given their lives to You. I confess I often think about my own game plan and not Yours. Help me to be truly committed to You this week. Show me one thing I can do to love You better in my school. Amen.

Around the Word This Week

Each day this week, read a verse and respond to it however you want. Think about it. Write it down on an index card that you can carry with you. Journal about it. Share it with a friend. Pray that the verse will impact you and you will obey it. It's your choice. To get you started thinking about how the Scripture relates to your life, consider the question that follows it.

⭐ DAY 2

"Jesus replied, 'All who love me will do what I say. My Father will love them, and we will come and make our home with each of them.'"   John 14:23

What do you think prevents Jesus from making His home in your heart?

★ DAY 3

"Those who obey God's word truly show how completely they love him. That is how we know we are living in him. Those who say they live in God should live their lives as Jesus did."

1 John 2:5-6

How do we know we're truly living for Jesus? When Jesus was on earth, how did He live?

 **DAY 4**

"Commit everything you do to the LORD. Trust him, and he will help you." Psalm 37:5

What have you kept back from God?

 ## DAY 5

"Commit your actions to the Lᴏʀᴅ, and your plans will succeed."

Proverbs 16:3

What plans do you need to take to God today?

Over the Weekend

"Seek the Kingdom of God above all else, and live righteously, and he will give you everything you need."   Matthew 6:33

What keeps you from believing God will supply everything you need?

WEEK FIVE
Sin and Pain

 DAY 1

"He personally carried our sins in his body on the cross so that we can be dead to sin and live for what is right. By his wounds you are healed. Once you were like sheep who wandered away. But now you have turned to your Shepherd, the Guardian of your souls."   1 Peter 2:24-25

ELLIE HAD AN AWFUL WEEK. It all started at band practice when one of her "friends" made fun of her. "Ellie dresses like someone who shops in a thrift store. With those hand-me-downs, she'll never be popular," Sandi told the entire band. Ellie steered clear of the girls as much as possible because they teased her.

Ellie planned her own revenge, though. Sandi had confided in her about her parents' upcoming divorce and asked

Ellie to keep it to herself. To get back at Sandi, Ellie told as many people as she could about Sandi's home situation.

The following week at band practice the director, Mrs. Krikorian, witnessed the girls arguing. She pulled both girls aside to get to the bottom of their dispute.

"She said I dress like I shop in a thrift store," Ellie said, glaring at Sandi.

"Whatever!" Sandi crossed her arms. "Ellie did something worse to me. She told my secret to the world. Now everyone knows about my parents' divorce!"

Mrs. Krikorian calmed the girls down. "You both need to say you're sorry." She made each girl apologize to the other before they were allowed to leave. Still, Ellie left feeling just as angry at Sandi, and not sorry at all. She forgot about Jesus' ability to take care of her sin and the sin of others.

Jesus bears the weight of our sin, whether it is making fun of what people wear or lying or cheating or breaking a promise. Because He died on the cross for our sins, we don't need to live with sin. We don't need to do things that hurt other people. We can experience true and lasting forgiveness.

But look what else the apostle Peter says. Jesus' wounds heal us. The wounds Ellie received from Sandi and the other girls will heal if she puts her trust in Jesus. Jesus is both the sin bearer and the pain bearer—He covers our sins and comforts us when others sin against us. Talk about an amazing God!

✎ Take Action

Have you ever hurt someone because that person hurt you first? What would have happened if you had remembered, in that moment, that Jesus bore your sin and the sin of others against you? Would you have done something different? Look for opportunities this week to confess your sin to Jesus. And if you're hurt, bring Him your pain, too. He will bear both.

✝ Connect with Jesus

Jesus, I fail a lot. I say and do things I shouldn't. Please forgive me. And help me remember that when I'm hurt by someone else's sin, I can run directly to You. Help me feel You when I'm hurting. Amen.

Around the Word This Week

Each day this week, read a verse and respond to it however you want. Think about it. Write it down on an index card that you can carry with you. Journal about it. Share it with a friend. Pray that the verse will impact you and you will obey it. It's your choice. To get you started thinking about how the Scripture relates to your life, consider the question that follows it.

★ DAY 2

"He heals the brokenhearted and bandages their wounds."

Psalm 147:3

Who in your life needs to be healed by God?

⭐ DAY 3

"If we confess our sins to him, he is faithful and just to forgive us our sins and to cleanse us from all wickedness."

1 John 1:9

When was the last time you confessed your sins to God?

⭐ DAY 4

"But he was pierced for our rebellion, crushed for our sins. He was beaten so we could be whole. He was whipped so we could be healed. All of us, like sheep, have strayed away. We have left God's paths to follow our own. Yet the LORD laid on him the sins of us all." Isaiah 53:5-6

How does it make you feel knowing that Jesus took on all your sins, the ones you committed last year, the ones you'll do today, and all your future sins?

⭐ DAY 5

"Watch yourselves! If another believer sins, rebuke that person; then if there is repentance, forgive. Even if that person wrongs you seven times a day and each time turns again and asks forgiveness, you must forgive." Luke 17:3-4

Why is it so hard to forgive someone who keeps hurting you?

Over the Weekend

"Get rid of all bitterness, rage, anger, harsh words, and slander, as well as all types of evil behavior."   Ephesians 4:31

Have you ever been bitter? What effect did that bitterness have on you?

 DAY 1

"It was in the year King Uzziah died that I saw the Lord. He was sitting on a lofty throne, and the train of his robe filled the Temple. Attending him were mighty seraphim, each having six wings. With two wings they covered their faces, with two they covered their feet, and with two they flew. They were calling out to each other, 'Holy, holy, holy is the LORD of Heaven's Armies! The whole earth is filled with his glory!'"

Isaiah 6:1-3

CASEY HAD A SERIOUS crush on a pop singer. She downloaded every song of his and covered the walls of her room with posters of him. His face adorned her pillowcase. Only her best friend, Ashley, knew that every night she kissed her idol before falling asleep.

In January, the singer's website ran an essay contest to determine his biggest fan. Casey wrote and rewrote her five-hundred-word entry. She asked her mother to read it, then her English teacher. Both of them thought she had done a good job. When Casey finally clicked the submit button, she worried that the essay wouldn't win. After all, thousands of girls had entered.

A month later, she received a telephone call.

"Is this Casey Johnston?" the caller asked.

"Yes, this is she," Casey answered.

"I'm happy to inform you that you've won the essay contest. A limousine will pick you up on Thursday for a day with your favorite singer!"

Casey nearly fainted. She asked several questions to make sure this was real, but when the caller asked to talk to her mom, she realized her dream had come true.

When Thursday came, Casey couldn't contain herself. Butterflies fluttered in her stomach. She was going to meet her pop idol face-to-face! After walking through a barricade and being searched by his bodyguards, Casey went up to him and shook his hand. He kissed her cheek. Then she stood nearby and watched him rehearse for the show.

Casey's obsession with the pop singer is a small picture of what our awe for God should look like. According to the Old Testament prophet Isaiah in today's verses, God is a great ruler. He is important. And His talents are more amazing than the best singer ever. Thankfully, we don't have to win a contest to gain His attention for a few hours. Although He is holy and

His glory is spectacular, He wants you to be near Him every minute of every day. You are a VIP in His eyes!

 Take Action

Write a fan letter to God. Tell Him why you love Him. What excites you the most about Him? Why do you want to be around Him?

✝ Connect with Jesus

Jesus, I sometimes forget how amazing You are, how holy. I don't always understand that You are big and important. Please forgive me for forgetting. I praise You this week that You are my glorious Ruler who loves me. Amen.

Around the Word This Week

Each day this week, read a verse and respond to it however you want. Think about it. Write it down on an index card that you can carry with you. Journal about it. Share it with a friend. Pray that the verse will impact you and you will obey it. It's your choice. To get you started thinking about how the Scripture relates to your life, consider the question that follows it.

★ DAY 2

"When I look at the night sky and see the work of your fingers— the moon and the stars you set in place—what are mere mortals that you should think about them, human beings that you should care for them?"   Psalm 8:3-4

The last time you looked at the night sky, how did it make you feel? How did it make you feel about God?

★ DAY 3

"O Sovereign LORD, you have only begun to show your greatness and the strength of your hand to me, your servant. Is there any god in heaven or on earth who can perform such great and mighty deeds as you do?"   Deuteronomy 3:24

When has God done something great and mighty in your life? In your family's life?

⭐ DAY 4

"Yours, O Lord, is the greatness, the power, the glory, the victory, and the majesty. Everything in the heavens and on earth is yours, O Lord, and this is your kingdom. We adore you as the one who is over all things. Wealth and honor come from you alone, for you rule over everything. Power and might are in your hand, and at your discretion people are made great and given strength."   1 Chronicles 29:11-12

What does it mean to adore God? How do you adore Him?

⭐ DAY 5

"Look up into the heavens. Who created all the stars? He brings them out like an army, one after another, calling each by its name. Because of his great power and incomparable strength, not a single one is missing." Isaiah 40:26

Does knowing God made every single thing in the universe comfort you? Why?

Over the Weekend

"They will speak of the glory of your kingdom; they will give examples of your power. They will tell about your mighty deeds and about the majesty and glory of your reign. For your kingdom is an everlasting kingdom. You rule throughout all generations."   Psalm 145:11-13

What does "kingdom" mean to you? How is God the King of your life?

WEEK SEVEN
Filthy Lips

⭐ DAY 1

Last week you read about the Old Testament prophet Isaiah who stood in God's presence with angels all around shouting, "Holy, holy, holy." Here are the next two verses:

"Their voices shook the Temple to its foundations, and the entire building was filled with smoke. Then I said, 'It's all over! I am doomed, for I am a sinful man. I have filthy lips, and I live among a people with filthy lips. Yet I have seen the King, the LORD of Heaven's Armies.'" Isaiah 6:4-5

THE SWEAR WORD SLIPPED easily from Cameron's lips. And the positive response he got from his buddies made him feel good that he fit in. What did it matter what he said? Sure the word was dirty, but it felt cool to be one of the guys. And so he said the word again, then threw in a nastier one for good measure.

His longtime friend James walked by as Cameron said the words to his new group of friends. James raised his eyebrows at the second word. "I've never heard you talk like that."

"It's no big deal. I say it all the time," Cameron boasted. "What's the problem?"

James pulled Cameron aside. "What if your mom heard you say that?"

"How in the world would she ever hear?"

"What if I told her?" James crossed his arms over his chest.

"You wouldn't."

"You're right. I wouldn't. But I'm just looking out for you. It's not cool to swear."

Cameron shook his head. "What do you know? Are you saying that I'm not good enough for you anymore?"

"Just forget it. Never mind." James walked away.

Cameron rejoined his group of friends and let another word fly. But it didn't feel nearly as satisfying after James's words to him.

Like Isaiah says, we are all people with unclean lips. He's not talking about swearing here, although swearing isn't something that would please God. Isaiah is pointing out our tendency to sin with our mouths. We boast. We tear people down. We lie. We share others' secrets. In the presence of a holy God, we soon realize how unclean our mouths are. Isaiah felt this, felt the weight of his sin.

The good news is that God, while He is holy, has made a way for us to have clean mouths (and hearts). He sent His Son, Jesus, to make a way for us to be clean and free.

✎ Take Action

The next time you're in the grocery store or at the gas station, read the headlines of the gossip magazines. How would you feel if someone followed you around, took your picture at crazy moments, and then wrote lies about you? Say a prayer for one of the celebrities whose picture is on the front page of one of the tabloids.

✟ Connect with Jesus

Jesus, I know I'm a person with unclean lips. I say things I shouldn't. I've told lies. I've gossiped. More than that, I've thought awful thoughts about people. Please clean me from the inside out. I want my words to make You smile.

Around the Word This Week

Each day this week, read a verse and respond to it however you want. Think about it. Write it down on an index card that you can carry with you. Journal about it. Share it with a friend. Pray that the verse will impact you and you will obey it. It's your choice. To get you started thinking about how the Scripture relates to your life, consider the question that follows it.

 **DAY 2**

"My lips will speak no evil, and my tongue will speak no lies."

Job 27:4

When was the last time someone lied to you? What happened? How did it make you feel?

★ DAY 3

"Who may worship in your sanctuary, Lord? Who may enter your presence on your holy hill? Those who lead blameless lives and do what is right, speaking the truth from sincere hearts. Those who refuse to gossip or harm their neighbors or speak evil of their friends."   Psalm 15:1-3

Why is it important for you to speak truth to your friends?

 **DAY 4**

"If you claim to be religious but don't control your tongue, you are fooling yourself, and your religion is worthless."

James 1:26

When was the last time you regretted something you said? What did you do about it?

 **DAY 5**

"The Scriptures say, 'If you want to enjoy life and see many happy days, keep your tongue from speaking evil and your lips from telling lies.'" 1 Peter 3:10

Why do you think it hurts so much when someone says something mean about you? About others?

Over the Weekend

"I said to myself, 'I will watch what I do and not sin in what I say. I will hold my tongue when the ungodly are around me.'"

Psalm 39:1

How can you be gracious and kind to those who say unkind things?

⭐ DAY 1

Last week you read about Isaiah, an Old Testament prophet who realized he had an unclean mouth. Now read what happened next:

"Then one of the seraphim flew to me with a burning coal he had taken from the altar with a pair of tongs. He touched my lips with it and said, 'See, this coal has touched your lips. Now your guilt is removed, and your sins are forgiven.' Then I heard the Lord asking, 'Whom should I send as a messenger to this people? Who will go for us?' I said, 'Here I am. Send me.'"

Isaiah 6:6-8

EACH MONTH DANIELA'S PARENTS, along with other families from their Sunday school class, traveled an hour away to a large city to make dinner for and hang out with people with AIDS. Daniela heard her parents and her older brother, Aidan, talk about how much fun they had eating dinner, playing games, and sometimes even dancing with the patients. But Daniela was afraid. What if she got infected? What if the people were scary?

Instead of voicing her concerns with her family, Daniela made an excuse about too much homework. She stayed home. Every time she thought she had enough nerve to go, her fear stopped her and she made another excuse.

But after her best friend, Sierra, went and told Daniela all about it, Daniela decided to try it and see for herself. Everyone acted friendly. She ate pizza and salad with the residents and served peach cobbler. She listened to one woman tell how she ended up on the street when she was Daniela's age because her stepfather kept threatening her. When the music started, Daniela chose to learn a new dance. She laughed. She didn't want to leave.

Many of us are like Daniela. We fear doing something different or scary or out of our comfort zone. We don't want to take risks. We like our safe lives. But sometimes God calls us to do radical things. He sees our hurting world (yes, even the world within your school), and asks, "Who will I send?"

Consider answering like Isaiah did, enthusiastically saying, "Here I am, God. Send me." You might be surprised to find that serving God in difficult or strange places will change your heart and life forever.

✎ Take Action

Go on your church website and look up ministries that the church is doing. Find out what church-related activities your parents are involved in. Pray about what God wants you to do, and then obey Him, even if it's scary.

✝ Connect with Jesus

Jesus, I like my comfortable, easy life. Forgive me. Please show me where I can step out and be radical for You. I want to be able to say, "Here I am. Send me." Help me to get there, Jesus. Amen.

Around the Word This Week

Each day this week, read a verse and respond to it however you want. Think about it. Write it down on an index card that you can carry with you. Journal about it. Share it with a friend. Pray that the verse will impact you and you will obey it. It's your choice. To get you started thinking about how the Scripture relates to your life, consider the question that follows it.

★ DAY 2

"Don't just listen to God's word. You must do what it says. Otherwise, you are only fooling yourselves."   James 1:22

What are some specific ways you can do what God's Word says?

★ DAY 3

"I have come down from heaven to do the will of God who sent me, not to do my own will."   John 6:38

When was the last time you did your own will and not God's? What was the result?

 **DAY 4**

"I take joy in doing your will, my God, for your instructions are written on my heart." Psalm 40:8

Who in your life seems to love to do what God asks?

⭐ DAY 5

"Moses and the Levitical priests addressed all Israel as follows: 'O Israel, be quiet and listen! Today you have become the people of the Lord your God. So you must obey the Lord your God by keeping all these commands and decrees that I am giving you today.'"   Deuteronomy 27:9-10

Why is it hard to obey God?

Over the Weekend

"Not everyone who calls out to me, 'Lord! Lord!' will enter the Kingdom of Heaven. Only those who actually do the will of my Father in heaven will enter."   Matthew 7:21

How can you obey God this week? What decisions do you face that might change if you obey Him?

 ## DAY 1

"How good it is to be near God! I have made the Sovereign
LORD my shelter, and I will tell everyone about the wonderful
things you do."   Psalm 73:28

WHEN GINNY FIRST spied Robert cheating in class, she won-
dered if she should say anything. She had studied hard for
the math test, losing hours of sleep to memorize formulas,
so seeing Robert with the numbers written on his hand made
her blood boil. But Robert was popular. And cute. And very
powerful. If he found out she tattled on him, her reputation
would suffer. So she let it go.

   The next week, Robert cheated again, this time passing
out little cheat sheets to his soccer teammates before class.
While Ginny struggled to remember the jumbled numbers

in her head, nearly half of the class had the answers at their fingertips. Still, she kept quiet, fearing the consequences.

Three days later, Robert had the answers for the following day's exam. Ginny noticed him taking one of the master tests sitting on Mr. Hiles's desk when he was out of the room. Ginny decided to tell. She trembled when she approached Mr. Hiles after school, then spilled the whole story. She couldn't help crying.

"You did the right thing," Mr. Hiles said. "But I've known about Robert for a few weeks now, and I planted those tests. I commend you for your honesty."

Ginny nodded. "But if he finds out you know, I'm sure he'll trace it back to me."

"Leave that to me," Mr. Hiles said. "I'll handle it."

The next day, Mr. Hiles called Robert to his desk, and with a voice loud enough so the class would hear, he said, "Robert, I know you've been cheating for weeks. I purposely left the test answers here to see what you'd do. You've given me the proof I need to give you the grade you deserve." He handed Robert back his test paper with a giant red F written at the top. Because Mr. Hiles acknowledged that he trapped Robert, he protected Ginny from being Robert's target.

We all need protection, don't we? We need someone like Mr. Hiles to shelter us from the attacks of others. We need a safe place, a safe person. Did you know God is a safe place? The psalmist who wrote today's verse realized that God listens to everything we pour out to Him, even our secrets or the things we struggle with. He will keep things quiet. His shoulders are big enough to carry our worries. When He does that we can't help but tell others how awesome He is. So run to Him today. Let Him protect you.

✎ Take Action

Grab a pen and paper and write out a prayer to God, telling Him everything you're thinking right now. Give Him everything you are stressing over. Ask Him to shelter you and keep you safe. Thank Him for having big shoulders.

✝ Connect with Jesus

Jesus, I need You to shelter me, to protect me. Sometimes I'm afraid. Sometimes I'm confused. Sometimes I'm just plain tired and need Your strength. Please listen to my prayer today and come near. I need You beside me. Amen.

Around the Word This Week

Each day this week, read a verse and respond to it however you want. Think about it. Write it down on an index card that you can carry with you. Journal about it. Share it with a friend. Pray that the verse will impact you and you will obey it. It's your choice. To get you started thinking about how the Scripture relates to your life, consider the question that follows it.

★ DAY 2

"Do not be afraid or discouraged, for the LORD will personally go ahead of you. He will be with you; he will neither fail you nor abandon you."   Deuteronomy 31:8

How does this verse encourage you?

⭐ DAY 3

"The eternal God is your refuge, and his everlasting arms are under you."   Deuteronomy 33:27

How does knowing God's arms are underneath you help you cope with the stress of your life this week?

⭐ DAY 4

"I know the LORD is always with me. I will not be shaken, for he is right beside me. No wonder my heart is glad, and I rejoice. My body rests in safety."   Psalm 16:8-9

Does this verse describe the attitude of someone you know? In other words, who in your life is not shaken by circumstances because he or she trusts God?

 # DAY 5

"God is our refuge and strength, always ready to help in times of trouble. So we will not fear when earthquakes come and the mountains crumble into the sea. Let the oceans roar and foam. Let the mountains tremble as the waters surge!"

Psalm 46:1-3

Why would it be scary to be in an earthquake? How could knowing God help you endure one?

Over the Weekend

"As soon as I pray, you answer me; you encourage me by giving me strength." Psalm 138:3

Keep track of God's answers to the list of concerns you wrote down in your prayer earlier this week.

WEEK TEN
Serve like a Dog

 DAY 1

"The greatest among you must be a servant. But those who exalt themselves will be humbled, and those who humble themselves will be exalted." Matthew 23:11-12

CASH LOVED HIS DOG, PIPPIN. Everywhere Cash went, Pippin followed. And when Cash went to sleep, Pippin curled up on the floor beside his bed.

When Cash had to have surgery, Pippin stayed near him when he came home. He curled up next to Cash's bed, seeming to will his friend back to health. One night after everyone went to bed, Cash developed a raging fever. Pippin barked and barked until Cash's mom came in the room and took his temperature. She had Cash take a cool shower, then they went to the emergency room. The doctor said, "I'm glad you brought him in. He has an infection."

Cash's mom believed Pippin saved her son's life.

When Cash finally recovered, Pippin stood there, wagging his tail, begging for a walk.

Jesus wants us to serve others the way Pippin served Cash. Here are three ways we can do that.

We must be available. Pippin stayed near Cash. In the same way, we need to stay close to our friends and family so we know their needs and can be there when life gets difficult. Being available is a part of serving.

We must be fascinated. To really love and serve others, we must become so familiar with who they are that we recognize when something's not right. Pippin knew Cash so well that he understood when something was terribly wrong. If we are to serve others, we must make a huge effort to know how they will react or feel even before they tell us.

We must be steady. Pippin didn't leave his friend's side, even when Cash couldn't play with him or walk him. One of the best ways to serve your friends is to affirm them. Doing so may not necessarily benefit you directly, but it will greatly benefit your friendship.

Serving others, Jesus says, also involves being humble. It means we put others first, above our needs or wants. It means we don't think we're too good to serve a "nerdy" person or someone who is often overlooked at school.

✎ Take Action

If you have a dog, when you take your pet for a walk today thank God for the example of faithfulness and service your dog gives you. If you don't have a dog, see if a neighbor or friend will let you take their dog for a nice long walk.

✝ Connect with Jesus

Jesus, help me to be a servant. I want to be available to my friends. I want to be attuned to everything about them. I want to serve them and know them better. Help me to put them first and be humble enough to do that this week. Oh, and please send me someone new I can serve, no matter who they are or what they look like. Amen.

Around the Word This Week

Each day this week, read a verse and respond to it however you want. Think about it. Write it down on an index card that you can carry with you. Journal about it. Share it with a friend. Pray that the verse will impact you and you will obey it. It's your choice. To get you started thinking about how the Scripture relates to your life, consider the question that follows it.

⭐ DAY 2

"You see, we don't go around preaching about ourselves. We preach that Jesus Christ is Lord, and we ourselves are your servants for Jesus' sake." 2 Corinthians 4:5

What does it mean to be a servant? How can you serve your parents this week?

★ DAY 3

"Don't be selfish; don't try to impress others. Be humble, thinking of others as better than yourselves. Don't look out only for your own interests, but take an interest in others, too. You must have the same attitude that Christ Jesus had."

Philippians 2:3-5

Who is the most humble person you know? What makes that person humble?

⭐ DAY 4

"He [Jesus] got up from the table, took off his robe, wrapped a towel around his waist, and poured water into a basin. Then he began to wash the disciples' feet, drying them with the towel he had around him."   John 13:4-5

What would it be like to wash your best friend's feet? Would you be embarrassed to do it?

⭐ DAY 5

"The master was full of praise. 'Well done, my good and faithful servant. You have been faithful in handling this small amount, so now I will give you many more responsibilities. Let's celebrate together!'" Matthew 25:21

What "little things" are you responsible for in your life? Why is it important to obey even in ways others may not see?

Over the Weekend

"After washing their feet, he put on his robe again and sat down and asked, 'Do you understand what I was doing? You call me "Teacher" and "Lord," and you are right, because that's what I am. And since I, your Lord and Teacher, have washed your feet, you ought to wash each other's feet. I have given you an example to follow. Do as I have done to you. I tell you the truth, slaves are not greater than their master. Nor is the messenger more important than the one who sends the message. Now that you know these things, God will bless you for doing them.'" John 13:12-17

How can you serve a friend today?

WEEK ELEVEN
Pull-Away Prayer

 ## DAY 1

"Before daybreak the next morning, Jesus got up and went out to an isolated place to pray."   Mark 1:35

THINGS WEREN'T GOING so well at home since Janie's older sister left for college. Her parents constantly fought, so Janie busied herself with everything she could think of. She played tennis. And she made sure she studied hard and got good grades. She became the president of the foreign language club and volunteered at a nursing home—anything to avoid being home. At home, she'd escape into her room and do extra credit homework or watch her favorite TV shows on Hulu. Most of the time, she stayed behind the closed door of her bedroom, but even that didn't stop Janie from hearing her parents argue.

Janie got to the place where she had to have noise to mask her pain. Her iPod blared all the time. The TV chattered in the background when she was doing her homework. The only time she really thought about her life was in the shower. That's when the tears streamed down her cheeks. She knew she should pray and ask Jesus for help, but all she could do was cry and finish washing her hair so she could disappear into her noisy world.

Sometimes we're a lot like Janie. We may not have problems at home or things we're trying to drown out, but we've gotten used to a noisy world. Surrounded by that noise, we don't have to think about deeper things, about life, about what God might want to be saying to us.

Imagine what it would have been like to be Jesus on earth. Everywhere He went, crowds pressed in on Him. He was a pop star of His time, constantly being bombarded by people with their expectations and problems. When Jesus wanted to pray with His Father, He had to pull away from the crowds. He would find an isolated place and pour His heart out there.

If Jesus, the Lord of the whole world, needed to get away from the busyness of life to pray, how much more do we need to! Here are seven "places" where you can get away this week:

- *In the shower.* Ask God to clean your heart from the inside out.
- *On a walk.* Ask God to walk alongside you this week.

- *In the car or on the bus.* As the world rolls by, ask God to open up your eyes to the needs around you.
- *In your room.* Ask God to show you how much He loves you.
- *In a quiet moment in class.* Ask God to be the Lord of your mind.
- *In your backyard.* Look up at the night sky and ask God to help you see how big He is.
- *During the sermon at church.* Ask God to speak to you directly through the pastor's words.

✎ Take Action

Choose three of the places above and note what happens when you follow the instruction.

✝ Connect with Jesus

Jesus, I'm busy. I admit it. Please forgive me for running around like crazy, forgetting about You. Slow me down this week long enough to spend time with You. I do love You. Amen.

Around the Word This Week

Each day this week, read a verse and respond to it however you want. Think about it. Write it down on an index card that you can carry with you. Journal about it. Share it with a friend. Pray that the verse will impact you and you will obey it. It's your choice. To get you started thinking about how the Scripture relates to your life, consider the question that follows it.

★ DAY 2

"Be still, and know that I am God! I will be honored by every nation. I will be honored throughout the world. The Lord of Heaven's Armies is here among us; the God of Israel is our fortress." Psalm 46:10-11.

When was the last time you sat quietly in your room?

★ DAY 3

"As Jesus and the disciples continued on their way to Jerusalem, they came to a certain village where a woman named Martha welcomed him into her home. Her sister, Mary, sat at the Lord's feet, listening to what he taught. But Martha was distracted by the big dinner she was preparing. She came to Jesus and said, 'Lord, doesn't it seem unfair to you that my sister just sits here while I do all the work? Tell her to come and help me.' But the Lord said to her, 'My dear Martha, you are worried and upset over all these details! There is only one thing worth being concerned about. Mary has discovered it, and it will not be taken away from her.'"   Luke 10:38-42

What does it mean to be distracted by life? How have you been distracted this week?

⭐ DAY 4

"Be careful how you live. Don't live like fools, but like those who are wise. Make the most of every opportunity in these evil days." Ephesians 5:15-16

Looking ahead to the rest of the day, how can you make the most of it?

 **DAY 5**

"Whether you eat or drink, or whatever you do, do it all for the glory of God." 1 Corinthians 10:31

What does it mean to do something for the glory of God?

Over the Weekend

"Bend down, O LORD, and hear my prayer; answer me, for I need your help." Psalm 86:1

How has God helped you this week? What lesson have you learned?

 DAY 1

"The LORD detests lying lips, but he delights in those who tell the truth." Proverbs 12:22

SADIE DIDN'T WANT to tell lies. But she had to. If she told the truth about her math grades her parents would ground her forever. She didn't want that. She was relieved her mom couldn't figure out how to see her grades online, and she hid her test results and tried harder, on her own. But no matter what she did or how much she studied, she couldn't pull up her grades.

When Sadie's mom asked her how she was doing in math, she said, "Doing great, Mom. My last test was awesome!"

But after her mom left the room, Sadie felt sick to her stomach. The truth? She had failed her last test, and her final grade in the class was a C-. Still, she kept up the deception until she lied so much she didn't know what was the truth anymore.

Then her teacher, Mrs. Snow, called Sadie's mom. Sadie could tell by the tone of her mom's voice that she knew the truth.

"Sadie, why didn't you tell me about what's been going on in math?"

At first Sadie started to tell another lie, but her mom interrupted. "Don't lie to me. Tell the truth. It'll be better if you do."

When Sadie spilled the entire story, she felt two things at the same time: shame for lying, and relief for finally telling the truth.

The Bible is clear about lying. In fact, lying is one of the Big Ten (Ten Commandments). Why does God hate lying? Because it hurts you and others. And it doesn't reflect Him at all since He is the God of truth. When you lie, it binds you up. The more you lie, the harder it is to remember what you've told to whom. Keeping up with your stories is exhausting.

God wants you to have a joyful life. But you can't have that if you're trapped by lies. Decide today to come clean—first to God, then to the people you've lied to.

✎ Take Action

In your first step toward a more truthful life, jot down a lie you remember telling recently. Imagine you decide to fess up. What do you say? How do you think your friends or family will respond? What is the worst thing that can happen? The best? Compose a prayer, asking God to help you tell the truth in this situation.

✝ Connect with Jesus

Jesus, I don't want to have lying lips. I don't want to be a liar. It's tiring and scary, and worst of all, it displeases You. I don't want to live a lie, brag about what's not true, or tell stories about others. Help me to tell the truth this week, even when it hurts. Amen.

Around the Word This Week

Each day this week, read a verse and respond to it however you want. Think about it. Write it down on an index card that you can carry with you. Journal about it. Share it with a friend. Pray that the verse will impact you and you will obey it. It's your choice. To get you started thinking about how the Scripture relates to your life, consider the question that follows it.

★ DAY 2

"Get the truth and never sell it; also get wisdom, discipline, and good judgment."   Proverbs 23:23

How do you find and get truth? Wisdom? Discipline? Good judgment?

⭐ DAY 3

"Jesus told him, 'I am the way, the truth, and the life. No one can come to the Father except through me.'"   John 14:6

Why do you think Jesus called Himself the truth?

⭐ DAY 4

"For you are the children of your father the devil, and you love to do the evil things he does. He was a murderer from the beginning. He has always hated the truth, because there is no truth in him. When he lies, it is consistent with his character; for he is a liar and the father of lies." John 8:44

How does the devil lie? What kinds of lies does he say to you?

⭐ DAY 5

"Instead, we will speak the truth in love, growing in every way more and more like Christ, who is the head of his body, the church." Ephesians 4:15

Have you known someone who spoke truthfully, but not lovingly? What happened?

Over the Weekend

"I will not allow deceivers to serve in my house, and liars will not stay in my presence."   Psalm 101:7

Why would it be hard to live with a liar?

 ## DAY 1

"We know how much God loves us, and we have put our trust in his love. God is love, and all who live in love live in God, and God lives in them." 1 John 4:16

BRADEN DIDN'T "GET" LOVE. His parents and grandparents loved him and all, but at school he felt left out and alone. As the new kid in an unfamiliar city and school, he often ate lunch by himself in the cafeteria. Though he prayed someone would place their tray next to him, his request seemed to hit the ceiling of the cafeteria, never making it to God's ears. Braden thought, *God doesn't love me either.*

Three weeks of lonely lunches passed. Then one day Corey

approached Braden. "Hey," he said, "wanna eat lunch with me and my friends?" He motioned over to a table bustling with laughter.

At first Braden thought Corey was pulling something over on him. But when the others waved him over, he decided to risk it. Thankfully, he had a great lunch and met some new guys. During the rest of the school year, Corey and Braden became close friends.

Have you ever felt lonely like Braden? Like no one cared?

Did you know Jesus is like Corey? (Or actually, Corey is like Jesus.) Jesus went out of His way, leaving His perfect home in heaven to come to this crazy earth, in order to befriend us, to invite us to eat with Him. That's what love is. It's sacrifice. It's going out of your way. It's taking a risk, but still pursuing.

God loves you that much.

He notices you that much.

He invites you today to truly understand what love is. Not just the fake love you see in movies with all the mush and romance, but God's real love that pursues you, your heart, your life. The more you accept God's love for you, the less insecure and needy you'll be. You'll live as though you are wildly loved by God.

✎ Take Action

On a sticky note write, "God loves me." Put it somewhere you'll see it every day.

✝ Connect with Jesus

Jesus, it's hard for me to understand what it means that You love me. Help me really understand. More than that, help me feel Your love in a new and surprising way this week. Would You please show me that You love me? Amen.

Around the Word This Week

Each day this week, read a verse and respond to it however you want. Think about it. Write it down on an index card that you can carry with you. Journal about it. Share it with a friend. Pray that the verse will impact you and you will obey it. It's your choice. To get you started thinking about how the Scripture relates to your life, consider the question that follows it.

★ DAY 2

"Christ will make his home in your hearts as you trust in him. Your roots will grow down into God's love and keep you strong. And may you have the power to understand, as all God's people should, how wide, how long, how high, and how deep his love is. May you experience the love of Christ, though it is too great to understand fully. Then you will be made complete with all the fullness of life and power that comes from God."   Ephesians 3:17-19

Why is it hard to truly understand God loves you? What prevents you from truly believing He loves you?

⭐ DAY 3

"God showed his great love for us by sending Christ to die for us while we were still sinners."   Romans 5:8

What surprises you about what God did?

★ DAY 4

"God loved the world so much that he gave his one and only Son, so that everyone who believes in him will not perish but have eternal life."   John 3:16

Imagine what it would be like to give your only child as a sacrifice for someone else. How would that feel? How does God's sacrifice of His Son show you He loves you?

 **DAY 5**

"This is real love—not that we loved God, but that he loved us and sent his Son as a sacrifice to take away our sins."

1 John 4:10

What does it mean that Jesus sacrificed His life for our sins?

Over the Weekend

"Such love has no fear, because perfect love expels all fear. If we are afraid, it is for fear of punishment, and this shows that we have not fully experienced his perfect love. We love each other because he loved us first."   1 John 4:18-19

Why do you think love shouldn't involve fear?

WEEK FOURTEEN
BFF

 DAY 1

"But Ruth replied, 'Don't ask me to leave you and turn back. Wherever you go, I will go; wherever you live, I will live. Your people will be my people, and your God will be my God. Wherever you die, I will die, and there I will be buried. May the LORD punish me severely if I allow anything but death to separate us!'" Ruth 1:16-17

CAMILLE AND PAIGE had been best friends since they were toddlers in the church nursery. Neither of them could remember not being with the other. Their friends called them "the twins." Both had short brown hair. They wore the same brand of jeans, used the same makeup, and played the same sports.

Then Kyle came into their lives. When Kyle asked Camille to hang out with him, she was thrilled at his attention. What she didn't know was that Paige wanted to spend time with Kyle too. Suddenly their relationship changed. Paige stopped talking to Camille. She even dropped out of lacrosse, their favorite sport.

"What gives?" Camille said to Paige, running to catch up with her.

"Nothing," Paige said.

"Don't say that. It's not nothing. What did I do?"

"Whatever." Paige turned away from Camille.

Camille started crying. "I'm sorry for whatever I did."

Paige turned back. "Stop spending so much time with Kyle and things will be fine."

"Why?"

Paige rolled her eyes and walked away.

Even the best of friendships can have stress and conflict. Maybe you're going through a time like that right now. Look back over Paige and Camille's conflict. What could Paige have done differently? What should Camille do now?

Naomi and Ruth, a mother-in-law and a daughter-in-law in the Old Testament, show us something important about friendships: faithfulness. Ruth promised to be there for Naomi, no matter what she faced. It's not always easy to be that kind of friend, particularly when our friends do things we don't like or spend time with the person we like. Even so, we can look to Jesus as the perfect example of friendship. He sticks with us even during the times we turn away from Him.

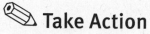 ## Take Action

Think of someone you've had a conflict with in the past month. Find your favorite cookie recipe (try AllRecipes.com to search for some yummy ones) and make a batch for your friend. Just because.

☦ Connect with Jesus

Jesus, friendships are hard sometimes. I'm hurt. I can't figure out why my friend treated me that way. Help me to forgive and move on. Help me to be a great friend to my friends. I want to be faithful like You. Amen.

Around the Word This Week

Each day this week, read a verse and respond to it however you want. Think about it. Write it down on an index card that you can carry with you. Journal about it. Share it with a friend. Pray that the verse will impact you and you will obey it. It's your choice. To get you started thinking about how the Scripture relates to your life, consider the question that follows it.

⭐ DAY 2

"Jonathan made David reaffirm his vow of friendship again, for Jonathan loved David as he loved himself."   1 Samuel 20:17

Who is your closest friend? How has that friendship changed over the past year?

⭐ DAY 3

"If someone says, 'I love God,' but hates a Christian brother or sister, that person is a liar; for if we don't love people we can see, how can we love God, whom we cannot see? And he has given us this command: Those who love God must also love their Christian brothers and sisters." 1 John 4:20-21

When was the last time you saw someone be really kind to another person? What happened?

★ DAY 4

"A friend is always loyal, and a brother is born to help in time of need."   Proverbs 17:17

Who is the most loyal friend you know? Why is being loyal important?

⭐ DAY 5

"Never pay back evil with more evil. Do things in such a way that everyone can see you are honorable. Do all that you can to live in peace with everyone."   Romans 12:17-18

When has it been hard for you to live in peace with someone?

Over the Weekend

"As iron sharpens iron, so a friend sharpens a friend."

Proverbs 27:17

What friend has helped you grow the most?

 ## DAY 1

"Jesus was deeply troubled, and he exclaimed, 'I tell you the truth, one of you will betray me!'" John 13:21

"I DON'T WANT ANYONE to know I'm adopted," Chelsea told her new friend Amanda at lunch.

"Your secret's safe with me." Amanda gathered her books and left their quiet corner.

For a few minutes, Chelsea worried about her secret being out there, but then she remembered how friendly and sweet Amanda had been to her the past several weeks. *Not to worry,* she thought.

It wasn't like it was a huge secret or anything. But Chelsea didn't feel like broadcasting it to the world quite yet. Her parents were still walking her through the news. Part of her wished her parents had told her many years ago, but another part felt like she was finally old enough to understand.

The next day at school, Toby, one of her closest guy friends, approached her. He looked mad. "Um, why didn't you tell me?"

"Tell you what?" Chelsea asked.

"Right. You told Amanda you're adopted and you didn't tell me?"

Chelsea backed up until she hit the locker behind her. "What?"

"Don't you think I'd want to know that?" Toby stormed off.

Tears dripped down Chelsea's cheeks. She didn't know what to do. And she certainly had no idea what she'd say to Amanda when she saw her.

In one of this week's Scriptures, you'll read how Jesus was tempted just the same way we are. He understands what it feels like to be let down by people, even betrayed by one of His very closest friends. Isn't it amazing that Jesus knew Judas would betray Him and yet He still chose him as one of His disciples? Jesus ate bread with Judas. They hung out together. They might have shared a laugh or two as they walked from town to town on dusty roads. And yet all the time Jesus knew this man, His friend, would turn Him over to people who wanted to kill Him.

Jesus can help us when we have been hurt greatly by our friends. We can ask Him to ease our anger and to give us the right words to say. Jesus provided forgiveness for each and

every person in the whole world when He died on the cross—
even His betrayer—so we can learn to forgive friends who
betray us. It's not easy or fun, but it is possible.

✎ Take Action

If you're currently dealing with someone who has betrayed
you, make time this week to talk to your parents or a youth
group leader about the situation. Ask what you should do
next. Be open to their advice, then pray that God would give
you the strength to do the next thing.

✝ Connect with Jesus

*Jesus, I don't like being betrayed by a friend. It hurts. I can't
imagine what it must have been like for You to have Judas betray
You. Please help me know what to do when I'm betrayed. Teach
me how to forgive. I need Your help, Jesus. Amen.*

Around the Word This Week

Each day this week, read a verse and respond to it however you want. Think about it. Write it down on an index card that you can carry with you. Journal about it. Share it with a friend. Pray that the verse will impact you and you will obey it. It's your choice. To get you started thinking about how the Scripture relates to your life, consider the question that follows it.

 DAY 2

"Judas Iscariot, one of the twelve disciples, went to the leading priests and asked, 'How much will you pay me to betray Jesus to you?' And they gave him thirty pieces of silver. From that time on, Judas began looking for an opportunity to betray Jesus."   Matthew 26:14-16

Why do you think Judas betrayed Jesus?

⭐ DAY 3

"This High Priest of ours understands our weaknesses, for he faced all of the same testings we do, yet he did not sin."

Hebrews 4:15

Jesus faced the same kinds of trials and temptations you face. What makes that truth encouraging to you?

⭐ DAY 4

"After saying these things, Jesus crossed the Kidron Valley with his disciples and entered a grove of olive trees. Judas, the betrayer, knew this place, because Jesus had often gone there with his disciples. The leading priests and Pharisees had given Judas a contingent of Roman soldiers and Temple guards to accompany him. Now with blazing torches, lanterns, and weapons, they arrived at the olive grove."   John 18:1-3

How do you think Jesus felt when He saw Judas betray Him?

 # DAY 5

"Don't befriend angry people or associate with hot-tempered people, or you will learn to be like them and endanger your soul." Proverbs 22:24-25

Why is this verse so true? Have you seen it happen?

Over the Weekend

"Wounds from a sincere friend are better than many kisses from an enemy." Proverbs 27:6

Why is it hard to receive a good friend's advice when the person is pointing out one of your sins?

 DAY 1

"All too quickly the message is crowded out by the worries of this life, the lure of wealth, and the desire for other things, so no fruit is produced." Mark 4:19

SAM WANTED AN IPHONE—BADLY. He pestered his parents about it, and he even neglected his own phone in hopes that he'd get the latest, greatest iPhone. But when the time came to renew the contract with his old phone, his parents didn't get him an iPhone. Sam threw a fit. He sulked and pouted and even did a terrible job mowing the lawn that week. Why couldn't his parents see that if he had that phone, he would finally be happy?

Later that week, he ran into his friend Joe at the skateboard park. "Whatcha been up to?" Joe asked.

"Nothing much." Sam noticed that Joe pulled out his phone and texted someone. "Except that my parents didn't get me the phone I wanted."

"So?" Joe shook his head, then put his phone back in his pocket.

"So, it's a big deal. I really want an iPhone."

"Do you know where I've been the past few weeks?" Joe asked.

"On some mission trip, right?" Sam kicked the ground.

"I went to this little church in Mexico, just across the border. I couldn't believe what I saw. The moment you cross the border, it's like another world. Kids without shoes, wearing torn clothes, kicking a soccer ball made of rags. It was wild."

"Sounds like it."

"Well, it changed me. Those kids laughed and played. They were happy even though they had nothing. I thought about everything I had, and how I wasn't as happy as they were. It made wanting a new gaming system seem really selfish."

Joe had learned a powerful lesson about the relationship between happiness and stuff. He realized that joy comes from loving life and knowing Jesus. True riches aren't the things we have, but the things we choose to do for Jesus. Jesus says we won't have fruitful lives if we whine about not having enough stuff. But if we learn to be content with what we have and stop focusing on what we don't have, we'll have more time and energy to serve others and love Him.

What would you rather have, more stuff or more of Jesus?

✎ Take Action

Get a large garbage bag and go through your room. Weed out what you don't use, need, or wear anymore. Ask your parents to take you to a Goodwill store or resale shop where you can donate items. Instead of replacing what you've given away, be content with everything you have.

✝ Connect with Jesus

Jesus, sometimes I get really caught up in what I want to wear, buy, and have. Please forgive me for thinking those things bring lasting happiness. I'm afraid that I won't grow if I constantly whine about not having enough. Help me to be content today with what I have. I want to be rich in You. Amen.

Around the Word This Week

Each day this week, read a verse and respond to it however you want. Think about it. Write it down on an index card that you can carry with you. Journal about it. Share it with a friend. Pray that the verse will impact you and you will obey it. It's your choice. To get you started thinking about how the Scripture relates to your life, consider the question that follows it.

★ DAY 2

"A person is a fool to store up earthly wealth but not have a rich relationship with God."   Luke 12:21

How can you have a rich relationship with God this week? What would that look like?

★ DAY 3

"Looking at the man, Jesus felt genuine love for him. 'There is still one thing you haven't done,' he told him. 'Go and sell all your possessions and give the money to the poor, and you will have treasure in heaven. Then come, follow me.' At this the man's face fell, and he went away sad, for he had many possessions." Mark 10:21-22

What one thing can you give away this week that would bless someone else?

★ DAY 4

"The world offers only a craving for physical pleasure, a craving for everything we see, and pride in our achievements and possessions. These are not from the Father, but are from this world." 1 John 2:16

Why do people struggle with wanting more and more and more?

⭐ DAY 5

"Here's the lesson: Use your worldly resources to benefit others and make friends. Then, when your earthly possessions are gone, they will welcome you to an eternal home." Luke 16:9

Who is the most giving person you know? Why do you think that person is like that?

Over the Weekend

"Sell your possessions and give to those in need. This will store up treasure for you in heaven! And the purses of heaven never get old or develop holes. Your treasure will be safe; no thief can steal it and no moth can destroy it."   Luke 12:33

When was the last time your family gave to someone in need? What happened?

 # DAY 1

"Summon your might, O God. Display your power, O God, as you have in the past." Psalm 68:28

DELIA FELT HELPLESS AT HOME. Her dad constantly got drunk and said all sorts of hurtful things to her, and yet her mom did nothing to stop it. In fact, sometimes her mom wasn't nice either. So when Delia got to school, she ruled it— through fear. She bullied others, particularly Theresa, who ran away every time she saw Delia in the hallway.

Delia wrote a mean note to Theresa, telling her to meet her after school at the baseball diamond so they could settle their differences. "You'd better bring some strong friends," she wrote.

Deep down, Delia didn't really want to bully others, but she couldn't help herself—it made her feel in control and formidable. When the end of the school day came, she sauntered out to the baseball diamond, thinking how she would scare Theresa.

Theresa came alone. She walked toward Delia with her eyes down and her hands behind her back. Then Theresa stopped a few feet in front of Delia.

"Ready?" Delia asked.

"No." Theresa's voice squeaked like a mouse. "I came to give you this." She pulled out a pink rose, tied with a white ribbon. "I thought you might like it."

At first Delia crossed her arms and tried to look mean, but then something strange happened. A stupid tear fell down her cheek. Then another. And another.

Theresa placed the flower at her feet and quickly walked away.

Some people think that being forceful with others is a sign of strength and power. But what Theresa did was much stronger. She faced hatred with love. She relied on God's power to do something totally surprising and beautiful. Every day we have a choice to rely on our own strength (or even try to create our own strength through bullying or putting others down) or trust in God's strength to help us love others. His strength is stronger than anything we can create on our own. And His strength changes the world, one life at a time.

✎ Take Action

Choose one of the Scriptures from this week and write it out on an index card. Place it on your bathroom mirror so you can be reminded of a strong God who is working on your behalf.

✝ Connect with Jesus

Jesus, I'm tired. I need Your strength. Forgive me for all the times that I've bullied someone. Help me to rely on Your strength to love my friends and my enemies. I can't do it alone. Amen.

Around the Word This Week

Each day this week, read a verse and respond to it however you want. Think about it. Write it down on an index card that you can carry with you. Journal about it. Share it with a friend. Pray that the verse will impact you and you will obey it. It's your choice. To get you started thinking about how the Scripture relates to your life, consider the question that follows it.

⭐ DAY 2

"I pray that from his glorious, unlimited resources he will empower you with inner strength through his Spirit."

Ephesians 3:16

What do you need God's amazing strength for today?

⭐ DAY 3

"The LORD is my strength and my song; he has given me victory. This is my God, and I will praise him—my father's God, and I will exalt him! The LORD is a warrior; Yahweh is his name!" Exodus 15:2-3

List seven things you can praise God for.

⭐ DAY 4

"There is no one like the God of Israel. He rides across the heavens to help you, across the skies in majestic splendor. The eternal God is your refuge, and his everlasting arms are under you." Deuteronomy 33:26-27

Why is there no one like God?

⭐ DAY 5

"The LORD is slow to get angry, but his power is great, and he never lets the guilty go unpunished. He displays his power in the whirlwind and the storm. The billowing clouds are the dust beneath his feet." Nahum 1:3

What does it mean that God is slow to get angry? How has God been patient with you?

Over the Weekend

"The Son radiates God's own glory and expresses the very character of God, and he sustains everything by the mighty power of his command. When he had cleansed us from our sins, he sat down in the place of honor at the right hand of the majestic God in heaven." Hebrews 1:3

What does it mean that God is majestic?

⭐ DAY 1

"Let someone else praise you, not your own mouth—a stranger, not your own lips." Proverbs 27:2

BEHIND HIS BACK, Brad's friends called him Brag. He constantly told his circle of friends about every single cool thing he did, bought, or experienced. And in the process, sometimes he put others down.

When Brad got an A+ on his science project and his friend Dale got a B-, Brad jumped all over it. "Hey, Dale, maybe you should've worked as hard as I did."

Dale went to his seat without answering.

Brad and Dale were sitting in math class when the teacher announced, "We have someone who got a perfect score on Friday's test."

Brad sat up straight. He knew it was him. So he blurted out, "You can save yourself the time, Mr. Shanks. We all know it was me who got the perfect score."

"Actually, no." Mr. Shanks walked past Brad and placed the test on Dale's desk. "Congratulations, Dale!"

Brad slumped back in his chair as he felt his face grow hot.

This week's verse says that it's better if we keep our mouths shut when it comes to our accomplishments. Instead, be quiet and see what God will do. Sometimes He chooses to shine the spotlight on us by having others praise us.

It's tiring to always be thinking of ourselves. And lonely, too. It can hurt other people's feelings and leave us without friends. The next time you're tempted to make a big deal about yourself, why not keep the words inside and look around you? Find someone doing something really cool and boast about that person to your friends. You'll find it's even more satisfying than bragging about yourself.

✏️ Take Action

One night this week at the dinner table brag about one of your family members. Be specific. "I really love that Mom spent so much time on this dinner. It's delicious." Open it up to everyone to respond and watch what happens.

✝ Connect with Jesus

Jesus, forgive me for bragging about myself. Help me to brag about You or other people. I want to be someone whom others want to be around, not because I'm cool but because I find ways to praise them. Help me change from being me-focused to others-centered—just like You are. Amen.

Around the Word This Week

Each day this week, read a verse and respond to it however you want. Think about it. Write it down on an index card that you can carry with you. Journal about it. Share it with a friend. Pray that the verse will impact you and you will obey it. It's your choice. To get you started thinking about how the Scripture relates to your life, consider the question that follows it.

★ DAY 2

"Fire tests the purity of silver and gold, but a person is tested by being praised." Proverbs 27:21

Why does the praise others give test us?

 # DAY 3

"They brag about themselves with empty, foolish boasting. With an appeal to twisted sexual desires, they lure back into sin those who have barely escaped from a lifestyle of deception." 2 Peter 2:18

What TV or movie character boasts the most?

⭐ DAY 4

"They are headed for destruction. Their god is their appetite, they brag about shameful things, and they think only about this life here on earth."   Philippians 3:19

When was the last time you heard someone brag about the bad things they did? How did that make you feel?

⭐ DAY 5

"The Scriptures say, 'If you want to boast, boast only about the Lord.'"   1 Corinthians 1:31

If you were to "boast only about the Lord," how would you do that?

Over the Weekend

"May the LORD cut off their flattering lips and silence their boastful tongues."   Psalm 12:3

How is flattering someone different from simply encouraging them?

 ## DAY 1

"God blesses those who are persecuted for doing right, for the Kingdom of Heaven is theirs."   Matthew 5:10

"WHAT KIND OF LUNCH IS THAT? What are you, a rabbit?"

Julia watched from the far end of the table as Kaylee made fun of Neeley during lunch. It made her stomach hurt to see it. She knew that she could either ignore what was happening or step in and stop it. She decided to pray quietly. As she did, she pictured Jesus there in the cafeteria. Of course! He would stand up for Neeley. So Julia decided to do it too.

"Kaylee?" Julia swallowed.

"Yeah, what?" Kaylee took a cracker from her lunch bag and pointed it at Neeley. "Are you on some kind of weird diet? Why do you only have carrot sticks?"

"Listen," Julia said, "who cares if Neeley eats carrots? Maybe she likes them. But I don't think she likes you bothering her."

Kaylee turned toward Julia. "Neeley doesn't mind, right, Neeley?"

Neeley's eyes were beginning to fill with tears as she looked at Julia to thank her for speaking up.

"She does mind," Julia said. "And it's not nice. Don't talk to her that way."

"What do you plan to do about it?" Kaylee asked.

"Leave the table." Julia stood.

"Feel free."

Julia grabbed her tray and found a lunch table in the corner.

Neeley followed her. "Thanks," she said. "You didn't have to do that. If someone crosses Kaylee, she gets back at that person."

Julia sighed. "I know. But I couldn't stand that she was messing with you like that."

Julia knows she probably will face Kaylee's revenge for doing the right thing. But she also believes that doing the right thing is what she's supposed to do, just as Jesus says. It's not easy, but Jesus will help her endure what Kaylee might do to her.

Even though it's hard to do the right thing (because there might be consequences), Jesus promises something huge to those who do. He gives them the Kingdom of Heaven! For those times when it seems your kingdom is crumbling in the lunchroom or classroom, take heart: Jesus sees you and will watch over you. He will give you grace and hope and peace in the midst of persecution. You'll know Him better because of it, and you'll have the deep satisfaction that you're doing exactly what He would do if He were standing there. God will be pleased if you stand up for someone who is being picked on, even if it doesn't please the bully doing it.

Take Action

With your parents' permission, log on to Persecution.com and learn about persecuted Christians around the world. Read one of the news stories at the top of the page. Then click on the "Pray" tab and pray for the first entry.

✝ Connect with Jesus

Jesus, I don't like to be persecuted for doing what is right. It's hard. Please help me be like You at school, at church, and at home. If persecution comes, help me to trust that You see me and You'll take care of me. I love You and need You. Amen.

Around the Word This Week

Each day this week, read a verse and respond to it however you want. Think about it. Write it down on an index card that you can carry with you. Journal about it. Share it with a friend. Pray that the verse will impact you and you will obey it. It's your choice. To get you started thinking about how the Scripture relates to your life, consider the question that follows it.

DAY 2

"You know how much persecution and suffering I have endured. You know all about how I was persecuted in Antioch, Iconium, and Lystra—but the Lord rescued me from all of it. Yes, and everyone who wants to live a godly life in Christ Jesus will suffer persecution." 2 Timothy 3:11-12

How has God rescued you from persecution lately?

★ DAY 3

"God will provide rest for you who are being persecuted and also for us when the Lord Jesus appears from heaven. He will come with his mighty angels."   2 Thessalonians 1:7

What do you think angels look like?

149

⭐ DAY 4

"Since they don't have deep roots, they don't last long. They fall away as soon as they have problems or are persecuted for believing God's word." Matthew 13:21

What will give you deep roots so you won't fall away from God?

⭐ DAY 5

"Do you remember what I told you? 'A slave is not greater than the master.' Since they persecuted me, naturally they will persecute you. And if they had listened to me, they would listen to you." John 15:20

How did people persecute Jesus?

Over the Weekend

"Can anything ever separate us from Christ's love? Does it mean he no longer loves us if we have trouble or calamity, or are persecuted, or hungry, or destitute, or in danger, or threatened with death?"   Romans 8:35

How would you answer the questions in Romans 8:35?

WEEK TWENTY
Home Life

 DAY 1

*"Children, obey your parents because you belong to the
Lord, for this is the right thing to do. 'Honor your father and
mother.' This is the first commandment with a promise: If
you honor your father and mother, 'things will go well for
you, and you will have a long life on the earth.' Fathers, do
not provoke your children to anger by the way you treat them.
Rather, bring them up with the discipline and instruction that
comes from the Lord."* Ephesians 6:1-4

ZAC SNEERED AT HIS MOM. "I don't care what you say. I'm
going to watch that show. Everyone I know watches it all the
time. Don't you have a sense of humor?"

"I don't like your tone, Zac." His mom stopped chopping
vegetables for that night's dinner and looked at him. "Your

dad and I have watched that show. It's too adult for you, and the humor is raunchy. Let it go. I'm tired of arguing with you."

Zac harrumphed. Then he sneaked off to his room, found the TV show online, and watched it. What harm would it do? Why were his parents so controlling? Besides, he always felt left out at school when his friends laughed about the crazy things the characters did and said.

Fifteen minutes later, Zac's mom brought laundry into his room to fold. She spied the show on Zac's laptop just as one of the characters made an off-color joke.

Zac thought he would die. His face turned red. *Why did Mom have to come in at that moment?*

Mom shook her head. "I see you're watching that show."

Zac still felt hot. "I didn't want to be the only one at school who didn't see it." But as he said the words, he felt small.

His mom extended her hand. "Your laptop. Hand it here."

"But—"

"For two weeks," she said. "Dad and I want to be able to trust you to watch appropriate shows, but you've shown us we can't."

The apostle Paul wrote that there are natural consequences for disobeying our parents. But one thing you may not know is that obeying your parents right now trains you to be a responsible adult later. You don't obey and respect your parents just because they're older than you. You do it because you love Jesus and you want to grow up to be a respectful adult. You obey because you realize your parents have your best interests at heart. Plus, if you obey now, things will be better for you later.

✎ Take Action

Ask your parents about what TV shows, movies, and songs they find offensive. Listen to their reasons why they're inappropriate. Choose to obey your parents and stay away from the things they warn you about.

✝ Connect with Jesus

Jesus, help me to obey and respect my parents. I want to do it to show I love You, and I also want to learn to be a respectful adult. Help me to realize that I'm in training right now for adulthood. Amen.

Around the Word This Week

Each day this week, read a verse and respond to it however you want. Think about it. Write it down on an index card that you can carry with you. Journal about it. Share it with a friend. Pray that the verse will impact you and you will obey it. It's your choice. To get you started thinking about how the Scripture relates to your life, consider the question that follows it.

⭐ DAY 2

"Wisdom belongs to the aged, and understanding to the old."

Job 12:12

How have your grandparents shown you they are wise? That they are understanding?

★ DAY 3

"Understand this, my dear brothers and sisters: You must all be quick to listen, slow to speak, and slow to get angry. Human anger does not produce the righteousness God desires." James 1:19-20

When have you been quick to listen? Slow to speak? Slow to get angry? When have you been the opposite?

★ DAY 4

"A wise child accepts a parent's discipline; a mocker refuses to listen to correction."   Proverbs 13:1

Why is it hard to listen when you are being disciplined?

⭐ DAY 5

"Be kind to each other, tenderhearted, forgiving one another, just as God through Christ has forgiven you." Ephesians 4:32

Who is God calling you to be tenderhearted toward? Is there someone you need to offer forgiveness to?

Over the Weekend

"Only a fool despises a parent's discipline; whoever learns from correction is wise." Proverbs 15:5

What does it mean to be a fool?

WEEK TWENTY-ONE
Grrrr

 DAY 1

"'Don't sin by letting anger control you.' Don't let the sun go down while you are still angry, for anger gives a foothold to the devil." Ephesians 4:26-27

KENNISHA SLAMMED HER DOOR. "Leave me alone!" she screamed.

Her sister, Clarice, knocked quietly. "I just want to say I'm sorry."

"You don't deserve to be in the same room with me." Kennisha threw a book across the room so hard that it made a mark on the wall.

Clarice took a deep breath. "I didn't mean to ruin your hair iron. It was an accident. I'm so sorry. I'll buy you a new one."

"You totally meant to ruin it. You're always taking my

things and breaking them." Kennisha opened the door and got in Clarice's face. "I wish you weren't my sister!"

Clarice stepped back, her eyes wet. "It really was an accident. And I don't take your things. If I do, I ask permission. Come on, let's just talk about it. I said I was sorry, and I'll replace it."

But Kennisha slammed the door again.

Clarice went to her room, flopped on the bed, and sobbed into her pillow.

Anger can destroy people. That's why Jesus equated hatred with murder. It kills others. Not only does it hurt our friends and family, but it makes our hearts bitter and hard. The more we allow anger to take over our lives, the less other people will want to be around us. Why? Because anger isolates.

In today's verses from Ephesians, the apostle Paul warns us not to let the sun go down on our anger. When we stuff our anger down and let it boil inside us, our hearts suffer. It's much better for our hearts (and our relationships) if we clear the air every single day. Don't hit the pillow tonight if you haven't resolved your anger with someone.

The Scripture also indicates that holding on to anger allows Satan to worm his way into your thoughts and actions. This is what "foothold" means. When we live in anger and keep letting the sun go down on our wrath, we give the devil a leg up in our lives.

✎ Take Action

The next time you feel yourself getting angry, take a moment to slow down, regroup, and pull away. Often in the midst of a heated situation, anger grows. Instead, step back. Write down your thoughts and everything that made you angry. Before the end of the day, ask Jesus to show you where you sinned. Be willing to confess your sin to the person you were angry with.

✝ Connect with Jesus

Jesus, I admit I can get super angry sometimes, and then things get out of control quickly. Help me to slow down, to regroup before I blow up. I don't want the sun to go down while I'm still angry, nor do I want to give the devil a leg up. Amen.

Around the Word This Week

Each day this week, read a verse and respond to it however you want. Think about it. Write it down on an index card that you can carry with you. Journal about it. Share it with a friend. Pray that the verse will impact you and you will obey it. It's your choice. To get you started thinking about how the Scripture relates to your life, consider the question that follows it.

⭐ DAY 2

"What is causing the quarrels and fights among you? Don't they come from the evil desires at war within you? You want what you don't have, so you scheme and kill to get it. You are jealous of what others have, but you can't get it, so you fight and wage war to take it away from them. Yet you don't have what you want because you don't ask God for it. And even when you ask, you don't get it because your motives are all wrong—you want only what will give you pleasure."

James 4:1-3

When was the last time you were jealous of what someone else had?

★ DAY 3

"May God, who gives this patience and encouragement, help you live in complete harmony with each other, as is fitting for followers of Christ Jesus. Then all of you can join together with one voice, giving praise and glory to God, the Father of our Lord Jesus Christ." Romans 15:5-6

How has God given you patience this week? Encouragement?

 **DAY 4**

"The LORD is compassionate and merciful, slow to get angry and filled with unfailing love." Psalm 103:8

What do you think a life of compassion looks like?

⭐ DAY 5

"An angry person starts fights; a hot-tempered person commits all kinds of sin." Proverbs 29:22

Why do you think hot-tempered people commit all sorts of sins?

Over the Weekend

"Stop being angry! Turn from your rage! Do not lose your temper—it only leads to harm." Psalm 37:8

When was the last time you lost your temper? What happened?

 ## DAY 1

"The people of Berea were more open-minded than those in Thessalonica, and they listened eagerly to Paul's message. They searched the Scriptures day after day to see if Paul and Silas were teaching the truth." Acts 17:11

"JESUS IS COMING BACK on February 18," Allison told her friend Josh. "So you'd better be ready."

"How do you know that?" Josh sat on the swing next to Allison at their neighborhood park.

"The Internet. This man has done all these calculations. He added up the days since Jesus died and matched them up with a bunch of prophecy from the Old Testament. I've read his stuff. It's really good."

"What are you going to do if Jesus doesn't come back on that day?" Josh asked.

Allison swung higher, her toes seeming to touch the blue sky. "He will. This guy's argument is very convincing."

"You can't believe everything you read on the Internet." Josh pumped higher, trying to reach Allison. "And besides, didn't Jesus say no one knows the day or the hour when He will return?"

"Where'd you hear that?"

"I didn't hear it. I read it in the Bible."

Josh would have fit right in with the believers in Berea described in the verse in Acts. They were the kind of people God wants us to be. They listened to a new teacher (Paul), but were unsure of what he taught. So they went back to the Bible to discover if Paul's words were true.

We need to follow that example. Sometimes we'll hear or read teaching that doesn't square with the Bible. When that happens, it's best to search the Bible to find out why the strange teaching doesn't fit. Ask your youth pastor or your parents if you're confused about a certain teaching. God's Word is the final authority.

✎ Take Action

Go to www.josh.org, click on the "Resources" tab, then scroll
down to "Watch and Listen." Click on the tab "Can I Trust
the Bible?" Choose one of the videos to watch. If you have
a chance, stop by each day this week. What did you learn
about the Bible that surprised you?

✝ Connect with Jesus

*Jesus, forgive me when I just assume everything that everyone
says about You is true. Help me to be a Berean, searching the
Bible to make sure what I'm hearing and reading is accurate.
Thank You for giving me Your Word to help guide me. Amen.*

Around the Word This Week

Each day this week, read a verse and respond to it however you want. Think about it. Write it down on an index card that you can carry with you. Journal about it. Share it with a friend. Pray that the verse will impact you and you will obey it. It's your choice. To get you started thinking about how the Scripture relates to your life, consider the question that follows it.

DAY 2

"Do not waste time arguing over godless ideas and old wives' tales. Instead, train yourself to be godly." 1 Timothy 4:7

Why isn't arguing productive?

★ DAY 3

"Then the way you live will always honor and please the Lord, and your lives will produce every kind of good fruit. All the while, you will grow as you learn to know God better and better." Colossians 1:10

What do you think it means to produce fruit in your life?

⭐ DAY 4

"There is much more we would like to say about this, but it is difficult to explain, especially since you are spiritually dull and don't seem to listen. You have been believers so long now that you ought to be teaching others. Instead, you need someone to teach you again the basic things about God's word. You are like babies who need milk and cannot eat solid food. For someone who lives on milk is still an infant and doesn't know how to do what is right. Solid food is for those who are mature, who through training have the skill to recognize the difference between right and wrong."

Hebrews 5:11-14

What does it mean to be a mature believer? How can you identify an immature believer? Would you call yourself immature or mature? Why?

⭐ DAY 5

"Then we will no longer be immature like children. We won't be tossed and blown about by every wind of new teaching. We will not be influenced when people try to trick us with lies so clever they sound like the truth." Ephesians 4:14

Why do you think some people are trying to trick us into believing wrong things about God?

Over the Weekend

"Don't let anyone think less of you because you are young. Be an example to all believers in what you say, in the way you live, in your love, your faith, and your purity. Until I get there, focus on reading the Scriptures to the church, encouraging the believers, and teaching them." 1 Timothy 4:12-13

Who has been a good example of a Christian in your life?

 ## DAY 1

"The night is almost gone; the day of salvation will soon be here. So remove your dark deeds like dirty clothes, and put on the shining armor of right living." Romans 13:12

OMAR LIKED PLAYING SUPER dark video games, the kind where you kill people and blood gushes everywhere. Sometimes he got so wrapped up in the games that he couldn't eat or sleep until he made it to the next level.

One day his friend Tyler came over to hang out. Omar greeted him, then quickly went back to his game. When he offered Tyler a chance to play, Tyler had a different suggestion. "Why don't we go outside and toss a Frisbee?"

Omar grunted and kept playing.

Tyler decided to take matters into his own hands. He

walked behind the entertainment unit and pulled the plug on Omar's game console.

"What in the world?" Omar growled. "I was just about to defeat an entire army!"

"That's not real," Tyler said. "I am. And I came over to hang out. So let's hang."

Omar didn't realize that when he lost himself in the world of violent video games, he dishonored not only his friend Tyler, but God as well. Romans 13:12 says to shed our dark deeds like we would smelly, dirty clothes, discarding the things in our lives that grieve God, our friends, and our family.

But it's not enough to just say no to the stuff that will harm us. We must replace it with the "shining armor of right living."

This week you'll be looking at Bible verses that talk about clothing. Remember that these verses are mostly symbolic. Ask yourself as you read them, "What do I need to remove from my life (with God's help)?" and "What is God asking me to wear this week?"

Here are some ideas:

- Take off sarcasm toward your parents and put on respect.
- Take off gossip and put on encouragement.
- Take off retreating into your room and put on hanging out with your family.

- Take off worrying about everything and put on trusting God to help you.
- Take off bitterness toward a friend and put on forgiveness.

✎ Take Action

Write down Ephesians 6:13-17, the last Scripture passage for this week, on an index card. Read it every day before you get dressed, reviewing the parts of God's armor that Paul mentions. Determine to tell the truth (the belt of truth), to do what's right (the breastplate of righteousness), to tell others about Jesus (gospel shoes), to have strong faith (the shield of faith), to rejoice that God has saved you (the helmet of salvation), and to faithfully read God's Word (the sword of the Spirit).

✝ Connect with Jesus

Jesus, forgive me for putting on the clothing of darkness, for doing things that don't please You. I'd rather do what brings glory to You. Help me be aware of how I'm living this week. I want to represent You well. Amen.

Around the Word This Week

Each day this week, read a verse and respond to it however you want. Think about it. Write it down on an index card that you can carry with you. Journal about it. Share it with a friend. Pray that the verse will impact you and you will obey it. It's your choice. To get you started thinking about how the Scripture relates to your life, consider the question that follows it.

★ DAY 2

"A final word: Be strong in the Lord and in his mighty power. Put on all of God's armor so that you will be able to stand firm against all strategies of the devil. For we are not fighting against flesh-and-blood enemies, but against evil rulers and authorities of the unseen world, against mighty powers in this dark world, and against evil spirits in the heavenly places."   Ephesians 6:10-12

What do you think are the "strategies of the devil"?

⭐ DAY 3

"Turning to his disciples, Jesus said, 'That is why I tell you not to worry about everyday life—whether you have enough food to eat or enough clothes to wear.'" Luke 12:22

Why do you think Jesus tells us not to worry about stuff?

★ DAY 4

"Don't be concerned about the outward beauty of fancy hairstyles, expensive jewelry, or beautiful clothes. You should clothe yourselves instead with the beauty that comes from within, the unfading beauty of a gentle and quiet spirit, which is so precious to God." 1 Peter 3:3-4

Who do you know who is beautiful on the inside?

★ DAY 5

"Because we belong to the day, we must live decent lives for all to see. Don't participate in the darkness of wild parties and drunkenness, or in sexual promiscuity and immoral living, or in quarreling and jealousy. Instead, clothe yourself with the presence of the Lord Jesus Christ. And don't let yourself think about ways to indulge your evil desires."

Romans 13:13-14

For you, what does it mean to live a decent life for all to see?

Over the Weekend

"Put on every piece of God's armor so you will be able to resist the enemy in the time of evil. Then after the battle you will still be standing firm. Stand your ground, putting on the belt of truth and the body armor of God's righteousness. For shoes, put on the peace that comes from the Good News so that you will be fully prepared. In addition to all of these, hold up the shield of faith to stop the fiery arrows of the devil. Put on salvation as your helmet, and take the sword of the Spirit, which is the word of God."   Ephesians 6:13-17

Why does faith in God stop the devil's attacks?

 DAY 1

"Be strong and courageous! Do not be afraid and do not panic before them. For the LORD your God will personally go ahead of you. He will neither fail you nor abandon you."

Deuteronomy 31:6

MARIA GROANED AFTER English class. How could she finish her assignment by tomorrow? Right now, she had soccer practice, followed by a meeting with the International Club. She didn't even know when she'd get dinner. Once she got home, she needed to complete a project that was due tomorrow but only half finished. Plus, her friend Darcy said she wanted to talk about this boy she liked. It was all too much.

When Maria finally got home, she gulped down a peanut

185

butter and jelly sandwich and stared at her project—a bridge constructed out of toothpicks and straws. She burst into tears.

"What's wrong?" her father asked.

"This stupid bridge is due tomorrow. I think I can finish it, but then I have this English paper to write. I'll never finish! And I'm so tired, I wish I could go to bed right now."

Her father sat beside her. "I can't write your paper for you, but at least I can help you finish the bridge."

"Thanks, Dad."

"No problem. But I'm worried about you. I think you're doing way too much. You need to remember not to spread yourself so thin. Tomorrow, let's go out for ice cream, and I'll help you decide what you can cut back on."

"I don't want to cut anything," she said.

Her father smiled. "We'll talk about it over ice cream."

Maria's life was overloaded. She didn't have time for rest or relaxation or even eating dinner with her family. Instead of asking God for help or finding out if her dad had some good solutions, Maria wanted to keep up her stressed-out life.

Today's verse from the Old Testament book of Deuteronomy promises something awesome: God will never leave you or turn His back on you—even when you're really stressed out. Prayerfully give your schedule to Him. Be careful, though. When we give God our schedules, He will probably ask us to sift out things. He wants us to be joyful and rested, something that is hard to be if we take on too many things.

✎ Take Action

Grab a piece of paper and write down everything you do in a week. Are you surprised by how long your list is? Now ask one or both of your parents to help you decide what needs to stay on your list and what needs to go. After that, spend some time in prayer giving all your stress to God. Thank Him that He won't walk away from you.

✝ Connect with Jesus

Jesus, forgive me for doing so much stuff that I forget You. I want to rely on You and not how much I can do. Please show me if I'm doing too much. Reveal what You want me to cut from my life. Help me to say no when You ask me to. Amen.

Around the Word This Week

Each day this week, read a verse and respond to it however you want. Think about it. Write it down on an index card that you can carry with you. Journal about it. Share it with a friend. Pray that the verse will impact you and you will obey it. It's your choice. To get you started thinking about how the Scripture relates to your life, consider the question that follows it.

⭐ DAY 2

"Give your burdens to the LORD, and he will take care of you. He will not permit the godly to slip and fall." Psalm 55:22

What burdens are bothering you today?

★ DAY 3

"The LORD helps the fallen and lifts those bent beneath their loads." Psalm 145:14

Have you ever felt bent beneath a heavy load? How did God help you?

⭐ DAY 4

"We are pressed on every side by troubles, but we are not crushed. We are perplexed, but not driven to despair. We are hunted down, but never abandoned by God. We get knocked down, but we are not destroyed."   2 Corinthians 4:8-9

Who do you know who keeps going, even when life gets hard?

⭐ DAY 5

"Jesus said, 'Come to me, all of you who are weary and carry heavy burdens, and I will give you rest. Take my yoke upon you. Let me teach you, because I am humble and gentle at heart, and you will find rest for your souls. For my yoke is easy to bear, and the burden I give you is light.'" Matthew 11:28-30

Can you remember the last time you really rested in Jesus? What did that feel like? If you've never rested in Him, what do you imagine that would be like?

Over the Weekend

"I heard a loud shout from the throne, saying, 'Look, God's home is now among his people! He will live with them, and they will be his people. God himself will be with them. He will wipe every tear from their eyes, and there will be no more death or sorrow or crying or pain. All these things are gone forever.'" Revelation 21:3-4

Why do you think God allows death, sorrow, crying, and pain in this life?

 ## DAY 1

"I carry in my heart the insults of so many people."

Psalm 89:50

As Emma looked in the mirror, Valerie's stinging words replayed in her mind.

"You're a big, fat pig."

Emma couldn't even remember why her "friend" said those awful words to her when they were eight years old, but it ended their friendship. Now, four years later, Emma rarely saw Valerie because she went to a different school. But Valerie's words stuck in her heart like superglue.

Even though what Valerie said wasn't true, over time Emma started believing it. She tried to watch what she ate. Some days she only munched on carrots and celery. Sometimes she was so hungry, she downed three Hot Pockets, then regretted it, and made herself throw up. She didn't want to become a big, fat pig. She exercised all the time, sometimes in secret, so her parents wouldn't guess what she was up to.

Even though the scale said she lost weight, every time she looked in the mirror, she saw a big, fat pig.

Have you ever had someone say something awful to you? Have you held those words close to your heart, so much so that those words still affect your actions today? Unfortunately, the truth is that people will hurt you. And sometimes they'll say terrible things behind your back or to your face.

But those insults don't have to haunt or define you. No matter what people tell you, you are wildly loved by God. He adores you. He thinks great thoughts about you all the time. Whenever you're tempted to rehash someone's awful words about you, say this out loud:

"I am wildly loved by the God of the universe."

Unfortunately, insults are a given in today's world. But God's love is a stronger given. Resting in His love will help you not only let go of the insults but also become a person who gives encouragement to others. As you remember what it felt like to be insulted, resolve by God's strength to become someone who praises your friends and seeks ways to build them up.

Imagine what your school would be like if everyone decided today to say positive things about each other instead of negative things!

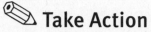 **Take Action**

The opposite of insulting someone is encouraging that person. So this week, grab a blank card and write a note of encouragement to someone who seems to need a lift. It can be a friend, a parent, a grandparent, a teacher—anyone who feels discouraged.

✝ Connect with Jesus

Jesus, I do carry an insult close to me. Help me remember that I am wildly loved by You. I don't want to be defined by someone else's mean words. I want to be free! Help me to encourage others this week, to use my mouth to build people up instead of tearing them down. Amen.

Around the Word This Week

Each day this week, read a verse and respond to it however you want. Think about it. Write it down on an index card that you can carry with you. Journal about it. Share it with a friend. Pray that the verse will impact you and you will obey it. It's your choice. To get you started thinking about how the Scripture relates to your life, consider the question that follows it.

★ DAY 2

"Don't let them scorn and insult me, for I have obeyed your laws."

Psalm 119:22

What insult do you remember?

⭐ DAY 3

*"I was given a thorn in my flesh. . . . Three different times
I begged the Lord to take it away. Each time he said, 'My
grace is all you need. My power works best in weakness.'"*

2 Corinthians 12:7-9

Why do you think the apostle Paul is happy to boast about
his weakess?

⭐ DAY 4

"A fool is quick-tempered, but a wise person stays calm when insulted." Proverbs 12:16

Who at your school remains calm when insulted? What has been the result of this response?

⭐ DAY 5

"He did not retaliate when he was insulted, nor threaten revenge when he suffered. He left his case in the hands of God, who always judges fairly."   1 Peter 2:23

Why do you think it's our natural reaction to want revenge when someone insults us?

Over the Weekend

"He will swallow up death forever! The Sovereign LORD will wipe away all tears. He will remove forever all insults and mockery against his land and people. The LORD has spoken!"

Isaiah 25:8

How does knowing that God will wipe away all your tears someday help you today?

⭐ DAY 1

"The LORD your God is living among you. He is a mighty savior. He will take delight in you with gladness. With his love, he will calm all your fears. He will rejoice over you with joyful songs." Zephaniah 3:17

CARLY LOVED TO SING. She wrote songs in her head at night, then jotted them down in the morning. Her favorite thing to do on the weekend: take her guitar to the dock at a nearby lake and write more songs. She wrote songs about friendship, or whatever she faced that week.

Soon people started noticing Carly and her original songs. Her friend Jay asked if she would write a song for his sister, Sophie, who battled leukemia. Because of chemo and radiation, Sophie didn't have the strength to get out of bed.

201

Carly wrote a song for Sophie with these words in the chorus:

You are beautiful
Just the way you are
Even if you don't do a single thing
You're loved, loved, loved anyway.

Whenever Carly visited, she sang that song to Sophie. Slowly, slowly, Sophie grew stronger. She got up. She walked. She eventually kicked the leukemia and hung out with her friends at school. She told everyone that a girl named Carly helped her heal.

The Old Testament minor prophet Zephaniah says some pretty cool things in today's verse. Did you realize that God loves you so much that He composes unique you-shaped songs and sings them over you? He is thrilled with everything about you because He made you. He rejoices that you are His child. Just like Carly showed love for her friend's sick sister, God loves you enough to sing over you.

The verse says some other pretty awesome things too:

- He lives among you and your family.
- He is mighty.
- He is a savior.
- He takes delight in you with gladness.
- His love will calm your fears.

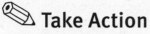 Take Action

Try writing a short song or a poem about someone you love. Then tuck it in an envelope and hand it to them. What a way to bless a friend!

✝ Connect with Jesus

Jesus, I can't believe You love me so much that You sing over me. Wow! Thank You. Help me to really, really, really believe that. Sometimes I forget how amazing Your love is. Thank You for loving me. Amen.

Around the Word This Week

Each day this week, read a verse and respond to it however you want. Think about it. Write it down on an index card that you can carry with you. Journal about it. Share it with a friend. Pray that the verse will impact you and you will obey it. It's your choice. To get you started thinking about how the Scripture relates to your life, consider the question that follows it.

⭐ DAY 2

"I led Israel along with my ropes of kindness and love. I lifted the yoke from his neck, and I myself stooped to feed him."

Hosea 11:4

How has God been sweet and gentle with you this past month?

⭐ DAY 3

"His unfailing love toward those who fear him is as great as the height of the heavens above the earth. He has removed our sins as far from us as the east is from the west. The LORD is like a father to his children, tender and compassionate to those who fear him." Psalm 103:11-13

Why do you think God is tender toward us? Compassionate?

⭐ DAY 4

"The faithful love of the LORD never ends! His mercies never cease. Great is his faithfulness; his mercies begin afresh each morning."   Lamentations 3:22-23

How does knowing God's mercy is brand-new every morning help you deal with what you face today?

⭐ DAY 5

"Satisfy us each morning with your unfailing love, so we may sing for joy to the end of our lives."   Psalm 90:14

Read what you've written over the last few weeks. Was there a morning or two when God reminded you of His love in a special way?

Over the Weekend

"You gave me life and showed me your unfailing love. My life was preserved by your care." Job 10:12

How has God preserved one of your family members' lives?

WEEK TWENTY-SEVEN
Search

 DAY 1

"The LORD is good to those who depend on him, to those who search for him. So it is good to wait quietly for salvation from the LORD. And it is good for people to submit at an early age to the yoke of his discipline." Lamentations 3:25-27

MALCOLM, THE SHORTEST in his circle of friends, volunteered to hide in the youth building for their annual game of Sardines. He could squeeze into the smallest spaces, so he found an empty trash can, curled up inside, and secured the lid. Five minutes passed. Then fifteen. Malcolm started sweating, then worrying. Would anyone find him? Would his friends give up and go, leaving him locked inside? He heard voices, but they seemed far away.

Just when Malcolm was about to burst with panic, Drake opened the trash lid and whispered, "Yes!"

Malcolm smiled. Of course it would be Drake, his best friend. He knew how Malcolm's mind worked, so it was easy to figure out where Malcolm was hiding. Now the trick was trying to stay hidden from the rest of the players. "Stay in there," Drake whispered, "and I'll hide behind the can."

God wants us to be like Drake. He wants us to search Him out, to find Him, to not give up until we know more about Him. The Old Testament prophet Jeremiah understood the vital importance of searching for God. God is good to those who search for Him.

Notice the words at the end of today's Scripture passage: "And it is good for people to submit at an early age to the yoke of his discipline." God's talking about you! The more you search for God and listen to His guidelines and discipline, the more you will grow and change to become more like Jesus.

It's important to realize that even though Jeremiah says we need to search for God, it doesn't mean that God isn't findable. The joy of searching for something or someone (like Drake did in the game of Sardines) is finding the thing or person you're looking for! The Scripture this week reminds us just how findable God is.

✎ Take Action

Round up several friends in your neighborhood for a game of hide-and-seek in a local park or large yard. (If you play at night, use flashlights.)

✝ Connect with Jesus

Jesus, I don't always search for You. Please forgive me for being so consumed with my own life and problems that I forget You are nearby, wanting to hang with me. I need You. Help me search for You today, tomorrow, and for the rest of this week. Amen.

Around the Word This Week

Each day this week, read a verse and respond to it however you want. Think about it. Write it down on an index card that you can carry with you. Journal about it. Share it with a friend. Pray that the verse will impact you and you will obey it. It's your choice. To get you started thinking about how the Scripture relates to your life, consider the question that follows it.

DAY 2

"'If you look for me wholeheartedly, you will find me. I will be found by you,' says the LORD."   Jeremiah 29:13-14

Why don't people look for God?

 # DAY 3

"Come close to God, and God will come close to you."

James 4:8

Are you encouraged to know that God will come close to you today? Why?

213

 # DAY 4

"You will search again for the LORD your God. And if you search for him with all your heart and soul, you will find him."

Deuteronomy 4:29

When have you lost something recently? Did you find it? Why is finding something so cool?

⭐ DAY 5

"The wicked are too proud to seek God. They seem to think that God is dead." Psalm 10:4

Why do you think proud people don't want to seek God?

Over the Weekend

"Plant the good seeds of righteousness, and you will harvest a crop of love. Plow up the hard ground of your hearts, for now is the time to seek the Lord, that he may come and shower righteousness upon you." Hosea 10:12

According to today's verse, when is the right time to seek the Lord?

WEEK TWENTY-EIGHT
Fraidy Cat

⭐ DAY 1

"He will cover you with his feathers. He will shelter you with his wings. His faithful promises are your armor and protection. Do not be afraid of the terrors of the night, nor the arrow that flies in the day. Do not dread the disease that stalks in darkness, nor the disaster that strikes at midday."

Psalm 91:4-6

CALLIE CONSTANTLY worries about every little thing. When she touches a door handle in a public restroom, she worries she'll get a disease. Five minutes before a test she starts shaking, even when she's fully prepared. When she walks home from school, the sound of every car scares her because she imagines someone jumping out and grabbing her. Most days she runs home, unlocks her front door, locks it behind her, then looks out the peephole to make sure no one has followed her.

She won't ride her bike with her friends, for fear of falling. She won't go to a movie unless her parents come along. She won't sleep over at a friend's house.

While we may not be as fearful as Callie, sometimes we live as if God isn't good or near. We forget that He runs the entire universe. Because of that, He can be trusted to protect us.

Does that mean that nothing bad will ever happen to you? No. In this crazy, upside-down world, things will go wrong. You'll get sick. Sometimes you'll fail a test. Rarely, but possibly, someone might chase you. You'll fall off your bike (or longboard or scooter or skis or surfboard). A movie might scare you. And you might find that the noises at a friend's house keep you awake at night, so you'd really prefer your own bed.

The good news is that God is there when you are afraid. He is near. Today's verses from the Psalms remind us that God is like a sweet mother hen, covering us with His feathers, protecting us from harm. He protects and shelters us.

Yes, things will go wrong. Life won't be pain-free. But we are never alone when these things happen. We do not need to live in fear of what could happen. Instead, we can hold on to God as He walks with us through the difficult times.

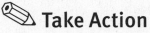 ## Take Action

Make a list of your biggest fears. Slip it into your Bible next to Psalm 91. The moment you start worrying about anything on your list, reread the psalm.

✝ Connect with Jesus

Jesus, sometimes I let fear nag me. I'm sorry. Help me to remember when I'm scared that You are nearby. I give You every single fear . . . fear of sickness, failing, loneliness. Please take all these fears and help me to live boldly and confidently today. Amen.

Around the Word This Week

Each day this week, read a verse and respond to it however you want. Think about it. Write it down on an index card that you can carry with you. Journal about it. Share it with a friend. Pray that the verse will impact you and you will obey it. It's your choice. To get you started thinking about how the Scripture relates to your life, consider the question that follows it.

⭐ DAY 2

"God has not given us a spirit of fear and timidity, but of power, love, and self-discipline."   2 Timothy 1:7

What is self-discipline? Why do you think God gives it to us?

★ DAY 3

"They do not fear bad news; they confidently trust the LORD to care for them." Psalm 112:7

Why does God care for us?

 **DAY 4**

"Don't be afraid of the people, for I will be with you and will protect you. I, the LORD, have spoken!"   Jeremiah 1:8

Have you seen God protect a friend? What happened?

⭐ DAY 5

"Don't be afraid of those who threaten you. For the time is coming when everything that is covered will be revealed, and all that is secret will be made known to all."   Matthew 10:26

How can we stop being afraid of people who threaten us?

Over the Weekend

"Don't be afraid of those who want to kill your body; they cannot touch your soul. Fear only God, who can destroy both soul and body in hell."   Matthew 10:28

What does it mean to fear God?

 DAY 1

"One of them, when he saw that he was healed, came back to Jesus, shouting, 'Praise God!' He fell to the ground at Jesus' feet, thanking him for what he had done. This man was a Samaritan. Jesus asked, 'Didn't I heal ten men? Where are the other nine? Has no one returned to give glory to God except this foreigner?'" Luke 17:15-18

MARK THREW THE MP3 PLAYER across the room. "This is not the one I wanted!" he shouted. "I wanted the one with more memory. I can't believe you didn't listen to me."

Mark's mom shook her head. "I'm sorry, honey, but that's what we could afford this year. With your father out of work, we've all had to make sacrifices." She picked up the MP3 player and put it in her purse.

"What are you doing?" Mark crossed his arms.

"You obviously don't want it. And you're not thankful for it, so I'll take it back. Even though it isn't as fancy as the one you wanted, it was still expensive. I'll return it and use the money to buy groceries."

"No! That's okay. I'll keep it." Mark grumbled.

"Sorry. If you can't be grateful, you can live without it."

Have you ever scowled about a gift you received? Most of us wouldn't overreact like Mark did, but sometimes we feel ungrateful for what we have. We forget to live a life of thankfulness.

In today's verses, we see the tail end of a miracle. Jesus healed ten lepers, and nine of them went on their way, not bothering to even say thanks. The tenth man, a Samaritan (an outcast and foreigner in Jesus' day), turned around the moment he was healed and ran flat out to Jesus, thanking Him. Jesus praised him for doing this.

Jesus wants us to practice being grateful for all the miracles He does in our lives. He also wants us to be grateful people, thanking others for their gifts, praying a prayer of thanks for our food, and being content with what we have from God's generous hands.

✎ Take Action

Every day this week, find someone to say thanks to. Maybe it will be the lunch lady who scoops food onto your plate, or a stranger who holds a door for you. Sometimes it's hardest to thank our parents or brothers and sisters. But watch how the dynamic of your family will change when you simply use two magic words—thank you.

✝ Connect with Jesus

Jesus, help me to be grateful for everything I have, including the air I breathe, the place I live, and the food in my stomach. Forgive me for not being content. Help me to say thank you to others this week. Thank You for loving me and blessing me with friends and family. Amen.

Around the Word This Week

Each day this week, read a verse and respond to it however you want. Think about it. Write it down on an index card that you can carry with you. Journal about it. Share it with a friend. Pray that the verse will impact you and you will obey it. It's your choice. To get you started thinking about how the Scripture relates to your life, consider the question that follows it.

★ DAY 2

"Since we are receiving a Kingdom that is unshakable, let us be thankful and please God by worshiping him with holy fear and awe." Hebrews 12:28

How can people show their awe for God?

 **DAY 3**

"[God] never changes or casts a shifting shadow."

James 1:17

Is it comforting to know that God never changes? Why?

★ DAY 4

"What do you have that God hasn't given you? And if everything you have is from God, why boast as though it were not a gift?"

1 Corinthians 4:7

What has God given you this week? How has He blessed you?

 **DAY 5**

"Giving thanks is a sacrifice that truly honors me. If you keep to my path, I will reveal to you the salvation of God."

Psalm 50:23

Who is the most grateful person you know? Why?

Over the Weekend

"He fills my life with good things. My youth is renewed like the eagle's!"　Psalm 103:5

What good things has God done in your family recently?

WEEK THIRTY
Turn Up Your Music

 DAY 1

"Sing a new song to the LORD, for he has done wonderful deeds. His right hand has won a mighty victory; his holy arm has shown his saving power!" Psalm 98:1

LISA BLASTED HER iShine music so loud her parents could hear it in the family room. Her mom came upstairs.

"Lisa, please turn the music down," she said.

"But it makes me feel so alive," Lisa said. "It really connects me to God. Just listen." She made room next to her on the bed.

"I will, but can you turn it down just a bit?"

"Sure, Mom." Lisa turned it down, then handed her mom the lyrics.

Her mom tapped her foot, then nodded. "This is catchy. And the lyrics are good. I can see why you like this."

Want to know something amazing? God created music. And He loves to hear it. Many of the psalms were written to be sung. In his letter to the believers in Ephesus, Paul urges them (and us!) to be "singing psalms and hymns and spiritual songs among yourselves, and making music to the Lord in your hearts" (Ephesians 5:19). What a wonderful gift!

There is so much music out there today that sometimes we can run into problems with our musical choices. How about your playlist? As you think about the songs you love, ask yourself:

- Do the lyrics honor God? Would I be embarrassed if my parents read the words?
- Have I made my music more important than my relationship with God? Does my world revolve around a specific song, group, or artist?
- When I play my music (and the speakers are on), do I respect my parents' instructions about the volume?

The psalm today reminds us that music is a gift God gives us, for release, for joy, for worship, for fun. Let's thank Him right now for that amazing gift.

✎ Take Action

Create a "worship God" playlist. Next time you're down or stressed, listen to your music, directing your praise to God. You'll be surprised at how that music will help turn your frown upside down!

✝ Connect with Jesus

Jesus, thank You for music. Help me to remember to sing praises to You when I'm having a hard time. Show me if my music honors You. Help me be respectful of my parents' musical boundaries. Amen.

Around the Word This Week

Each day this week, read a verse and respond to it however you want. Think about it. Write it down on an index card that you can carry with you. Journal about it. Share it with a friend. Pray that the verse will impact you and you will obey it. It's your choice. To get you started thinking about how the Scripture relates to your life, consider the question that follows it.

⭐ DAY 2

"Wake up, lyre and harp! I will wake the dawn with my song."

Psalm 108:2

What favorite song gets your morning off to a good start?

⭐ DAY 3

"David and all Israel were celebrating before God with all their might, singing songs and playing all kinds of musical instruments—lyres, harps, tambourines, cymbals, and trumpets." 1 Chronicles 13:8

What is your favorite instrument? Is there a group you like that plays different types of instruments?

⭐ DAY 4

"Praise his name with dancing, accompanied by tambourine and harp." Psalm 149:3

How can dancing be a form of worship? Why would God want us to dance before Him?

 **DAY 5**

"Sing a new song of praise to him; play skillfully on the harp, and sing with joy." Psalm 33:3

What words would be in your new song for God?

Over the Weekend

"David also ordered the Levite leaders to appoint a choir of Levites who were singers and musicians to sing joyful songs to the accompaniment of harps, lyres, and cymbals."

1 Chronicles 15:16

Why do you think David went to all this trouble for music?

DAY 1

*"My child, if sinners entice you, turn your back on them! . . .
My child, don't go along with them! Stay far away from their
paths."* Proverbs 1:10, 15

D'ANN'S CLOSEST FRIEND was Jessica. They shared everything
in their lives, especially secrets. They'd always made fun of
their friends who sneaked out for parties. "I will never do
that," Jessica told D'Ann too many times to count.

But three months ago, Jessica changed. She started hanging out with a rough crowd. At first D'Ann didn't mind since
they still spent time together. Then one day she noticed
Jessica's breath smelled like cigarettes.

"Have you been smoking?" D'Ann asked Jessica as they
sat in the park together.

241

"So what if I have?" Jessica became defensive.

"Why would you do that?" D'Ann looked at her.

"It's fun. And it's cool. Besides, it makes me feel happy."

D'Ann couldn't believe what her friend was saying. "You'll get addicted!"

"No, I won't. And I'll prove it to you." Jessica pulled out a pack of cigarettes and a lighter. She looked around, lit one, took a puff, then handed it to D'Ann. "Go ahead. Try it. You'll understand."

D'Ann stood up. "No!" She didn't know what else to do except walk away, tears beginning to fall down her cheeks.

D'Ann will have to make some difficult choices about how much time she'll spend with Jessica. While it's good to connect with friends, it's not always wise to spend a lot of time with friends who consistently make bad choices. Often the influence of a straying friend is greater than that of a friend who is trying to live right.

Today's verses from the book of Proverbs (which is smack-dab in the middle of your Bible) are pretty clear. Stay away from people who actively try to undermine your faith or entice you to sin.

[Note: This doesn't mean you can't be friends with people who don't know Christ. Read the rest of this week's verses. Most of the warnings in Scripture ask you not to associate with believers who try to lead you astray. We still need to love those who don't know Jesus.]

✏️ Take Action

For this activity, you'll need another person and a chair. You stand on the chair while your friend stands on the floor. Now grab your friend's hand and try to pull the person up onto the chair while your friend tries to pull you to the ground. What happened?

✝ Connect with Jesus

Jesus, I want to honor You in my friendships, but I'm confused. What should I do if one of my friends keeps trying to make me choose bad behavior? Help me to know when to stay close or walk away. I need Your help. Amen.

Around the Word This Week

Each day this week, read a verse and respond to it however you want. Think about it. Write it down on an index card that you can carry with you. Journal about it. Share it with a friend. Pray that the verse will impact you and you will obey it. It's your choice. To get you started thinking about how the Scripture relates to your life, consider the question that follows it.

★ DAY 2

"Don't be fooled by those who say such things, for 'bad company corrupts good character.'"   1 Corinthians 15:33

Has someone ever been a bad influence in your life or a friend's life?

⭐ DAY 3

"Walk with the wise and become wise; associate with fools and get in trouble." Proverbs 13:20

Why do you think hanging out with fools gets you in trouble? Have you ever had that happen?

★ DAY 4

"The temptations in your life are no different from what others experience. And God is faithful. He will not allow the temptation to be more than you can stand. When you are tempted, he will show you a way out so that you can endure."

1 Corinthians 10:13

Has God ever given you an opportunity to flee a sin? What did you do?

⭐ DAY 5

"You are not to associate with anyone who claims to be a believer yet indulges in sexual sin, or is greedy, or worships idols, or is abusive, or is a drunkard, or cheats people. Don't even eat with such people."   1 Corinthians 5:11

What does it mean to worship idols?

Over the Weekend

"Don't team up with those who are unbelievers. How can righteousness be a partner with wickedness? How can light live with darkness? What harmony can there be between Christ and the devil? How can a believer be a partner with an unbeliever?"   2 Corinthians 6:14-15

What's the difference between befriending those who aren't Christians and spending all your time with them?

 DAY 1

"Understand, therefore, that the LORD your God is indeed God. He is the faithful God who keeps his covenant for a thousand generations and lavishes his unfailing love on those who love him and obey his commands."   Deuteronomy 7:9

"I LOVE HOW GOD made this an amazing day. Just look at the clouds!" Siri smiled as she walked next to Jason during their game of Frisbee golf.

"You're making God up." Jason's words poked at Siri.

"No. He's real." Siri flung the Frisbee toward the next hole, wincing when it thwacked a tree.

Jason whirled his disc toward hole 4 for a near-perfect shot. "Prove it."

"Well," Siri said, "look at the sky. Someone had to make that, right?"

"That's not what my science book says. Don't tell me you believe all those stories about God and Adam and Eve."

Siri picked up her disc and whipped it toward the hole. "I do."

"You're crazy."

Later Siri thought about her conversation with Jason. She felt guilty for not convincing him about God, but she also felt unsettled. Was God real? Or did she just believe all that stuff because her parents said so? Or the pastor at her church? What if God wasn't real? What if everything she thought God created just happened?

You might think it's wrong for Siri to doubt like this, but doubts are actually quite normal, and God can handle our questions about Him. In fact, it's better that she search now and make her faith her own rather than shoving unanswered questions down deep. Guess what? God is big enough to shoulder your doubts. He is stronger than your questions. And He isn't taken by surprise when you wonder how He created the universe.

Moses wrote the book of Deuteronomy. In today's verse, Moses tells us that God is indeed God. He sits on His throne. He loves to reward those who seek Him and try to know Him and learn to trust Him.

God will help you share your faith in a natural way. It's not up to you to save your friends. Your job is to pray for them, let God know you're willing to share His love with them, and watch and see how God leads them.

Take Action

Ask one of your parents to play the role of Jason in the above story. Have them come up with as many questions and doubts about God as they can. See if you can figure out ways to respond. If you get stuck, ask your parent to switch roles with you and see how your dad or mom would respond.

Connect with Jesus

Jesus, sometimes I doubt. I don't have all the answers. And because I can't see You, it's hard for me to believe You're real sometimes. Help me to trust You. Please show Yourself to be real to me this week. And help me share You with my friends. Amen.

Around the Word This Week

Each day this week, read a verse and respond to it however you want. Think about it. Write it down on an index card that you can carry with you. Journal about it. Share it with a friend. Pray that the verse will impact you and you will obey it. It's your choice. To get you started thinking about how the Scripture relates to your life, consider the question that follows it.

★ DAY 2

"When the Father sends the Advocate as my representative—that is, the Holy Spirit—he will teach you everything and will remind you of everything I have told you."   John 14:26

Why do you think the Father sent us the Holy Spirit?

⭐ DAY 3

"We can't help but thank God for you, dear brothers and sisters loved by the Lord. We are always thankful that God chose you to be among the first to experience salvation— a salvation that came through the Spirit who makes you holy and through your belief in truth." 1 Thessalonians 2:13

Why is it important to believe the truth, according to this verse?

 **DAY 4**

"Anyone who wants to come to [God] must believe that God exists and that he rewards those who sincerely seek him." Hebrews 11:6

How does God reward people who seek Him?

★ DAY 5

"Then Jesus told him, 'You believe because you have seen me. Blessed are those who believe without seeing me.'"

John 20:29

Has there been a time when it has been hard for you to believe in Jesus?

Over the Weekend

"By faith we understand that the entire universe was formed at God's command, that what we now see did not come from anything that can be seen." Hebrews 11:3

Why do you think God created this world? Why did He create people to live on it?

 DAY 1

"What sorrow awaits you teachers of religious law and you Pharisees. Hypocrites! For you are like whitewashed tombs—beautiful on the outside but filled on the inside with dead people's bones and all sorts of impurity. Outwardly you look like righteous people, but inwardly your hearts are filled with hypocrisy and lawlessness." Matthew 23:27-28

JENNA FELT AWFUL EVERY time she hung out with Bekah, because Bekah teased her for being a Bible slacker. Bekah was the number one player on the youth group's Bible drill team and knew over 120 verses by heart. There were Bible verses plastered all over Bekah's bathroom mirror and she was always quoting new ones she memorized.

Yesterday Bekah shared a verse about gossip with Jenna.

Fifteen minutes later, Bekah said, "I can't stand Miriam on my team. She thinks she knows everything! She says she has more verses memorized than me, but I know she's just a liar. She says that her parents are helping and are behind her. But I know for a fact that her mom doesn't even live with her."

Jenna gasped, trying to decide what to say next. What she really wanted to do was to point out the obvious: Bekah was disobeying the very verse she had memorized! But Jenna held her tongue and simply said, "We should probably pray for Miriam. It must be really hard not to have her mom there."

All of us are hypocrites at some time or another. We don't always do what we say or act the way we should. Jesus reserved His harshest words for people who pretended to be super-religious but instead put on a show. He called them "whitewashed tombs." A tomb is a place for dead people. And whitewash is paint that appears white for a period of time, but then fades away.

In the same way, when we boast about how religious we are and then do the very thing we say we won't, it's as if we've whitewashed our dead hearts to make them seem vibrant. God knows our hearts and He wants them to be alive and willing to obey Him. Because of His death on the cross and resurrection from the grave, Jesus promises to make our hearts amazingly alive! We don't have to pretend when He's done such cool things inside of us.

If you want to avoid being a hypocrite, remember this simple truth: it's not what we say; it's what we do. And we can't do what's right if our hearts are far from Him.

✎ Take Action

At the beginning of the week, take a sheet of notebook paper and fold it in half from top to bottom. Every day, write down one belief you've said out loud to someone. On the other side of the fold, write whether you've lived out that belief.

✝ Connect with Jesus

Jesus, I don't want to be like a Pharisee, saying one thing and then doing another. That is disobeying You. I want my heart to be right, to be alive, not dead. I need You to help me. Thank You that You have made me brand new and given me a heart that wants to obey. I want to walk that way this week. Amen.

Around the Word This Week

Each day this week, read a verse and respond to it however you want. Think about it. Write it down on an index card that you can carry with you. Journal about it. Share it with a friend. Pray that the verse will impact you and you will obey it. It's your choice. To get you started thinking about how the Scripture relates to your life, consider the question that follows it.

 **DAY 2**

"We can tell who are children of God and who are children of the devil. Anyone who does not live righteously and does not love other believers does not belong to God."   1 John 3:10

Have you ever found it hard to love other Christians? Why or why not?

⭐ DAY 3

"You may think you can condemn such people, but you are just as bad, and you have no excuse! When you say they are wicked and should be punished, you are condemning yourself, for you who judge others do these very same things. And we know that God, in his justice, will punish anyone who does such things." Romans 2:1-2

According to this verse, what are the sure signs that someone is a hypocrite?

⭐ DAY 4

"Why worry about a speck in your friend's eye when you have a log in your own? How can you think of saying to your friend, 'Let me help you get rid of that speck in your eye,' when you can't see past the log in your own eye? Hypocrite! First get rid of the log in your own eye; then you will see well enough to deal with the speck in your friend's eye."   Matthew 7:3-5

Why should we look at our own lives first before we confront a friend about his or her actions?

★ DAY 5

"Since you judge others for doing these things, why do you think you can avoid God's judgment when you do the same things? Don't you see how wonderfully kind, tolerant, and patient God is with you? Does this mean nothing to you? Can't you see that his kindness is intended to turn you from your sin?"   Romans 2:3-4

How has God been kind and forgiving toward you?

Over the Weekend

"Do not judge others, and you will not be judged. For you will be treated as you treat others. The standard you use in judging is the standard by which you will be judged."

Matthew 7:1-2

How would your school look if people stopped judging each other?

WEEK THIRTY-FOUR
Finish Well

⭐ **DAY 1**

"Finishing is better than starting. Patience is better than pride."

Ecclesiastes 7:8

JARED PROMISED HIS mom that he'd clean his room over the weekend. But Monday came and his room still looked like a cyclone had blown through it.

"Why didn't you do what you said?" his mom asked at breakfast.

Jared poured himself a glass of milk. "Well, I had lots of stuff to do this weekend."

His mom set a plate of French toast in front of him. "Oh, like skateboarding with your friends? And swimming?"

Jared took a bite, then looked at his plate. "Point taken. I'm sorry."

"I don't care if I've made a good point. You need to understand that when you say you're going to do something, you do it. Don't promise and then not follow through."

Jared agreed. "Sorry, Mom," he said. "I'll do it today after school. I promise."

But his friend Chris called and invited him to paintball. And he couldn't resist.

When he came home, his room was perfectly clean—even the pile of chip bags and other garbage on his desk was gone, everything except a piece of paper. Jared went over and read the note. "Bill for housekeeping services: $50.00 and one week of being grounded."

It's wonderful to have ambitions to do great things, but we need to take care of everyday things too, like cleaning our rooms. No matter what the task, we need to follow through and finish well. Wise King Solomon wrote today's verse to emphasize just how important it is to complete what we start. If the second half of the verse has you puzzled, consider this: If we are boastful (showing our pride) about what we will do and yet we don't do it, we'll disappoint others. However, if we are patient and quietly finish what we've started, we'll bless others.

When you combine the excitement of starting things with the patience to complete them, you'll be successful and honor God.

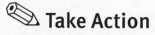 ## Take Action

Clean your room.

✝ Connect with Jesus

Jesus, sometimes I have so many ideas and activities and say that I'll do them all. But I can't. Help me to weed out the things in my life that overload it. And give me courage and patience to finish what I've started. And Lord? Forgive me for not cleaning my room or doing my chores. Amen.

Around the Word This Week

Each day this week, read a verse and respond to it however you want. Think about it. Write it down on an index card that you can carry with you. Journal about it. Share it with a friend. Pray that the verse will impact you and you will obey it. It's your choice. To get you started thinking about how the Scripture relates to your life, consider the question that follows it.

★ DAY 2

"Since we are surrounded by such a huge crowd of witnesses to the life of faith, let us strip off every weight that slows us down, especially the sin that so easily trips us up. And let us run with endurance the race God has set before us. We do this by keeping our eyes on Jesus, the champion who initiates and perfects our faith. Because of the joy awaiting him, he endured the cross, disregarding its shame. Now he is seated in the place of honor beside God's throne. Think of all the hostility he endured from sinful people; then you won't become weary and give up." Hebrews 12:1-3

How does knowing Jesus endured death on the cross help give you persistence?

⭐ DAY 3

"I have fought the good fight, I have finished the race, and I have remained faithful."   2 Timothy 4:7

When it comes to your relationship with God, what does it mean to fight the good fight?

 **DAY 4**

"I don't mean to say that I have already achieved these things or that I have already reached perfection. But I press on to possess that perfection for which Christ Jesus first possessed me. No, dear brothers and sisters, I have not achieved it, but I focus on this one thing: Forgetting the past and looking forward to what lies ahead, I press on to reach the end of the race and receive the heavenly prize for which God, through Christ Jesus, is calling us." Philippians 3:12-14

Is it hard to forget your past? Why or why not? What does it mean to look forward, especially this week? What situation in the past is holding you back from trusting God today?

 **DAY 5**

"My life is worth nothing to me unless I use it for finishing the work assigned me by the Lord Jesus—the work of telling others the Good News about the wonderful grace of God."

Acts 20:24

Ask God to show you someone to share Him with this week.

Over the Weekend

"Don't you realize that in a race everyone runs, but only one person gets the prize? So run to win! All athletes are disciplined in their training. They do it to win a prize that will fade away, but we do it for an eternal prize. So I run with purpose in every step. I am not just shadowboxing. I discipline my body like an athlete, training it to do what it should. Otherwise, I fear that after preaching to others I myself might be disqualified." 1 Corinthians 9:24-27

How is following Jesus like competing on a sports team?

 DAY 1

"Let all the world look to me for salvation! For I am God; there is no other. I have sworn by my own name; I have spoken the truth, and I will never go back on my word: Every knee will bend to me, and every tongue will confess allegiance to me."

Isaiah 45:22-23

"I CAN HANDLE IT," SHARA SAID. She stacked her books on the kitchen table, sat down, and looked at her father.

"No, you can't," her father said. "You postponed this paper until the last minute. How can you possibly write it? You've had half the school year to write it, and it's due tomorrow."

"Just watch me," Shara snapped.

She stayed up all night long, biting her nails, scribbling

out notes, writing her paper. When she finally hit "print," something wonky happened with her computer and the file. She lost everything!

Her father found her crying at the kitchen table the next morning. "What's wrong?"

"I thought I could do it. And I actually did, but the stupid computer ate my paper!"

Her father worked at the computer for a few minutes, was able to find a backup copy, and printed it off for her. But before he took her to school, he said, "How many gods are there in the universe?"

She looked at him like he was crazy. "What?"

"Just answer me," he said gently.

"Dad, there's only one God."

Her father smiled. "You're right. But last night you acted as if there were two. You and God."

"What do you mean?"

"God is the only One able to help us live our lives. When we try to control everything, it's almost like we're saying there are two Gods, us and Him."

In today's verses, the prophet Isaiah makes it very clear that there is only one God. Even though we say we believe that, sometimes our lives don't show it. We live in such a way that we are our own gods, attempting to control our lives. God wants us to recognize that there really is only one God and to praise Him.

✎ Take Action

Think about last week. When were you in charge of your life? What happened? How did you feel? Were you stressed? When did you live as if you believed there was only one God?

♱ Connect with Jesus

Jesus, forgive me for living in such a way that I forget You. I don't want to be a god. I want to love You and follow You first. Help me to see when I'm trying to control my life. Amen.

Around the Word This Week

Each day this week, read a verse and respond to it however you want. Think about it. Write it down on an index card that you can carry with you. Journal about it. Share it with a friend. Pray that the verse will impact you and you will obey it. It's your choice. To get you started thinking about how the Scripture relates to your life, consider the question that follows it.

 # DAY 2

"You alone are the LORD. You made the skies and the heavens and all the stars. You made the earth and the seas and everything in them. You preserve them all, and the angels of heaven worship you." Nehemiah 9:6

Imagine all the angels in heaven worshiping God. How would you describe what that looks and sounds like?

⭐ DAY 3

"This is what the LORD says—Israel's King and Redeemer, the LORD of Heaven's Armies: 'I am the First and the Last; there is no other God. Who is like me? Let him step forward and prove to you his power. Let him do as I have done since ancient times when I established a people and explained its future. Do not tremble; do not be afraid. Did I not proclaim my purposes for you long ago? You are my witnesses—is there any other God? No! There is no other Rock—not one!'"   Isaiah 44:6-8

How does knowing there is no other God encourage you today?

 **DAY 4**

"Then God gave the people all these instructions: 'I am the LORD your God, who rescued you from the land of Egypt, the place of your slavery. You must not have any other god but me.'"   Exodus 20:1-3

What does it mean to "have another god," rather than worshiping the one true God?

 **DAY 5**

"There is salvation in no one else! God has given no other name under heaven by which we must be saved." Acts 4:12

What are other ways people try to find God?

Over the Weekend

"But we know that there is only one God, the Father, who created everything, and we live for him. And there is only one Lord, Jesus Christ, through whom God made everything and through whom we have been given life."   1 Corinthians 8:6

What does it mean to truly live for Jesus?

WEEK THIRTY-SIX
Watered

 DAY 1

"The LORD will guide you continually, giving you water when you are dry and restoring your strength. You will be like a well-watered garden, like an ever-flowing spring."

Isaiah 58:11

WHEN RYAN COMPLETED the second part of the sprint triathlon he felt like a raisin, all dried up and dehydrated. He had started off strong, swimming a half mile, then hopping on his bike to race for the next twelve miles. The temperature was close to 100 degrees but Ryan rode hard. When he got off his bike, his thighs cramped. It took him a few hundred feet before his legs cooperated and he could complete his 5K run.

During the bike race, Ryan had forgotten to drink any water, thinking he could wait until the first water station during the 5K run. But it was farther along the course than Ryan remembered. When he finally saw it, he was limping, his mouth felt dry, and his vision was blurred. As he drank, most of it dribbled down his face. He had to stop a moment in the shade of the tent and drink slowly. A few minutes later, he continued racing.

When Ryan crossed the finish line, he collapsed. Paramedics rushed him into an ambulance and immediately gave him IV fluids and ice packs to cool him down. One of the paramedics asked him how much water he drank. Ryan admitted that he had waited until the last leg of the race. "That's not enough in this heat, son," the man said.

Ryan learned a valuable lesson about the importance of water on a hot day. In today's verse God promises to water us as if we were the greenest, most beautiful gardens on earth. He is that kind of God—one who keeps an eye on us and refreshes us.

Sometimes we get so caught up in our busy lives that we forget to stop and drink in God's goodness. The rest of this week's verses highlight Jesus as the One who gives us living water. He is the ultimate source! We will faint and grow sick spiritually if we forget to spend time with Him.

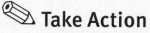 ## Take Action

Find a picture of a waterfall, river, lake, or the ocean and make it your desktop or phone background this week to remind you of the importance of water.

✝ Connect with Jesus

Jesus, thank You for being the fountain of living water. Help me understand what that means in my life. I want to be watered like a garden. Forgive me for forgetting to rest and spend time with You. Amen.

Around the Word This Week

Each day this week, read a verse and respond to it however you want. Think about it. Write it down on an index card that you can carry with you. Journal about it. Share it with a friend. Pray that the verse will impact you and you will obey it. It's your choice. To get you started thinking about how the Scripture relates to your life, consider the question that follows it.

★ DAY 2

"Anyone who believes in me may come and drink! For the Scriptures declare, 'Rivers of living water will flow from his heart.'" John 7:38

When was the last time you saw a river? How is a river different from a lake? Why do you think Jesus compares His presence to a river?

⭐ DAY 3

"I will pour out water to quench your thirst and to irrigate your parched fields. And I will pour out my Spirit on your descendants, and my blessing on your children. They will thrive like watered grass, like willows on a riverbank."

Isaiah 44:3-4

What would happen if you didn't have anything to drink for several days? How would your opinion about water change?

⭐ DAY 4

"Then the angel showed me a river with the water of life, clear as crystal, flowing from the throne of God and of the Lamb. It flowed down the center of the main street. On each side of the river grew a tree of life, bearing twelve crops of fruit, with a fresh crop each month. The leaves were used for medicine to heal the nations." Revelation 22:1-2

Draw the scene described in these verses.

 # DAY 5

"Is anyone thirsty? Come and drink—even if you have no money! Come, take your choice of wine or milk—it's all free!"

Isaiah 55:1

Why do you think God provides for people who follow Him?

Over the Weekend

"Jesus replied, 'If you only knew the gift God has for you and who you are speaking to, you would ask me, and I would give you living water.' 'But sir, you don't have a rope or a bucket,' [the woman at the well] said, 'and this well is very deep. Where would you get this living water? And besides, do you think you're greater than our ancestor Jacob, who gave us this well? How can you offer better water than he and his sons and his animals enjoyed?' Jesus replied, 'Anyone who drinks this water will soon become thirsty again. But those who drink the water I give will never be thirsty again. It becomes a fresh, bubbling spring within them, giving them eternal life.'"

John 4:10-14

How is Jesus' water better than plain old tap water? What kind of water is He referring to here?

 DAY 1

"When I discovered your words, I devoured them. They are my joy and my heart's delight, for I bear your name, O Lord God of Heaven's Armies." Jeremiah 15:16

NICOLE BURIED HER face deeper into the latest installment of her favorite book series. She didn't eat lunch, and only nibbled on cheese and crackers in her room instead of joining her family for dinner. When her mom came up to her room and asked if she was feeling all right, Nicole grunted, "Mom, can't you see I'm reading?"

The next day, Nicole saw the next book in the series at her school library and grabbed it before anyone else could. She stayed up most of the night, devouring the book.

The following morning, she made a beeline to the library. "Is the next book available?" she asked the librarian anxiously.

"Sorry," the librarian said. "It's checked out. But I can put you on a waiting list."

"But what will I read?" Nicole moaned.

After school, she asked her mom the same question. "What in the world can I read? I have to know what happens next!"

Her mom sat next to her on the couch. "You love stories, don't you?"

Nicole nodded.

Her mom handed her a Bible. "Then you'll love this."

"The Bible? Come on, Mom. Not that. I want a story!"

"The Bible is the most amazing story ever written."

Nicole shook her head. She left the Bible on the couch and went to her room.

It's not wrong to get lost in the pages of a great story. Stories speak to us. They take us to places we've never imagined and introduce us to people we've never met. And often, they teach us lessons about how to live.

Did you know the Bible is an amazing story? The Old Testament prophet Jeremiah loved this story so much that he ate it up. He couldn't get enough of God's story. There are hundreds of stories within the Bible's pages. Yet all of the stories together tell one epic adventure in the same way that The Lord of the Rings or The Chronicles of Narnia do.

The Bible is the story of people who turned their backs on

their King and hurt Him deeply. He banished them from His Kingdom. But eventually He sent His Son, the Prince, to make a peace treaty. The people beat up the Prince, then killed Him. Miraculously, He rose from the dead, surprising everyone. Because of His death and new life, the Son reunited the people with the King, making it possible to enjoy His blessings forever. How exciting is that?

Is it time to pull out your Bible and reread the story?

Take Action

Read the first few chapters of Genesis this week. It's how the story of God and you begins.

Connect with Jesus

Jesus, help me to read Your Word. I know it's important. Forgive me for looking at it as only a rule book. I want to read it as a dynamic adventure story. Help me to be swept away by God's Word this week. Amen.

Around the Word This Week

Each day this week, read a verse and respond to it however you want. Think about it. Write it down on an index card that you can carry with you. Journal about it. Share it with a friend. Pray that the verse will impact you and you will obey it. It's your choice. To get you started thinking about how the Scripture relates to your life, consider the question that follows it.

★ DAY 2

"All Scripture is inspired by God and is useful to teach us what is true and to make us realize what is wrong in our lives. It corrects us when we are wrong and teaches us to do what is right. God uses it to prepare and equip his people to do every good work." 2 Timothy 3:16-17

Write this verse on an index card and memorize it. Hang it someplace where you'll notice it every day.

★ DAY 3

"How can a young person stay pure? By obeying your word. I have tried hard to find you—don't let me wander from your commands." Psalm 119:9-10

When was the last time God brought a Bible verse to your mind? What happened? Which verse was it?

★ DAY 4

"For the word of God is alive and powerful. It is sharper than the sharpest two-edged sword, cutting between soul and spirit, between joint and marrow. It exposes our innermost thoughts and desires."   Hebrews 4:12

What can a good sword do? How is that similar to what the Bible does?

⭐ DAY 5

"Every word of God proves true. He is a shield to all who come to him for protection."   Proverbs 30:5

How has God been a shield for your family?

Over the Weekend

"I have hidden your word in my heart, that I might not sin against you."   Psalm 119:11

What does it mean to hide God's Word in your heart?

 DAY 1

"Don't let the excitement of youth cause you to forget your Creator. Honor him in your youth before you grow old and say, 'Life is not pleasant anymore.'" Ecclesiastes 12:1

"HEY, HELEN, WHY HAVEN'T I seen you in church the past month?" Melody asked.

Helen opened her locker. "I've been busy."

"Busy with what?"

"You know, just stuff. Shopping. Hanging with friends."

"I thought *I* was your friend." Melody adjusted her backpack.

"You are," Helen said. "It's just, I have these other friends who aren't so . . . how do I say it? Good."

They walked together to their next class while Melody

297

considered what she should say next. "Are you saying I act like I'm too good for you?"

"Yeah, sort of." Helen stopped. "It's just that I have my whole life to follow God, right? And now when I'm young I want to have fun. I don't want to worry about God hovering over me, telling me I'm bad."

"He doesn't do that!" Melody felt her throat tighten.

"Whatever. You can play around with all the boring people at church. Me? I'm going to have a blast. You're only young once."

Helen didn't realize the truth of today's verse, written by King Solomon. What seems exciting to her now will eventually lead her to forget God, make poor choices, and have regrets.

We may try to justify skipping church and spending less time with God and our Christian friends. But be warned: the longer you stay away from God and the further you run toward the world, the harder it is to come back and the more damage you'll do to yourself and those who love you.

Following Jesus while you're young is actually one of the most exciting, fulfilling, fun things you can experience.

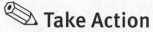 Take Action

Is there a person in your life whom you admire for his or her relationship with God? A person who follows Jesus well and sees it as an adventure? Text that person and tell why you admire him or her.

✝ Connect with Jesus

Jesus, I forget. I forget what You've done. And sometimes I forget how exciting it is to follow You. I don't want to walk away from You while I'm young. Keep me close to You right now. I love You. Amen.

Around the Word This Week

Each day this week, read a verse and respond to it however you want. Think about it. Write it down on an index card that you can carry with you. Journal about it. Share it with a friend. Pray that the verse will impact you and you will obey it. It's your choice. To get you started thinking about how the Scripture relates to your life, consider the question that follows it.

★ DAY 2

"Let all that I am praise the LORD; may I never forget the good things he does for me." Psalm 103:2

Sometimes it's hard to remember the great things God has done for us. Why do you forget?

★ DAY 3

"They did not keep God's covenant and refused to live by his instructions. They forgot what he had done—the great wonders he had shown them."   Psalm 78:10-11

What are God's instructions?

★ DAY 4

"If you look carefully into the perfect law that sets you free, and if you do what it says and don't forget what you heard, then God will bless you for doing it."   James 1:25

How has God blessed you when you've obeyed Him? What happened?

⭐ DAY 5

"Young people, it's wonderful to be young! Enjoy every minute of it. Do everything you want to do; take it all in. But remember that you must give an account to God for everything you do." Ecclesiastes 11:9

How does knowing you'll have to tell God everything you've done (even though He knows it already) help you act differently today?

Over the Weekend

"I will never forget your commandments, for by them you give me life." Psalm 119:93

How can God's commands give us life? How can disobeying them bring pain?

⭐ DAY 1

"Shadrach, Meshach, and Abednego replied, 'O Nebuchad-nezzar, we do not need to defend ourselves before you. If we are thrown into the blazing furnace, the God whom we serve is able to save us. He will rescue us from your power, Your Majesty. But even if he doesn't, we want to make it clear to you, Your Majesty, that we will never serve your gods or worship the gold statue you have set up.'" Daniel 3:16-18

RAY DIDN'T CONSIDER himself to be brave by any stretch of the imagination. He would have been embarrassed to admit to his friends that he was terribly afraid of heights. But one week, he did a brave thing.

He went to his friend Jagan's house one Saturday. They played basketball for several hours, then had a long lunch with Jagan's parents and younger sister. Though the food was different, Ray enjoyed it, particularly the chicken curry.

After lunch, Jagan invited Ray up to his room. He pointed to his closet. "This is where my gods are," he said.

Ray looked inside and saw several small metal statues. He smelled incense and noticed the smoldering wands in a holder.

Jagan handed Ray an incense wand. "Want to burn one to the god of the dying?"

For a moment, Ray held the incense. He didn't want to be insensitive to his friend, but at the same time he couldn't burn anything to a statue. It wasn't God! "I'm sorry," he said, "but I'm a Christian. I worship one God, and I don't think it would be right for me to light this to one of your gods."

Jagan seemed disappointed, but after a few minutes he and Ray were enjoying competing against each other on the Wii.

It's not likely we'll be asked to burn incense to a Hindu god like Ray was. But God does want us to be brave and unflinchingly loyal to Him. He promises to be with us, just as He helped the three men in today's verses. Shadrach, Meshach, and Abednego stood up to King Nebuchadnezzar and were willing to be burned alive for their beliefs. God chose to save them from the flames.

It's not always easy to be brave and stand up for our faith. It's hard to be courageous and say what we believe. But we do have the promise that God will be with us when we try.

✏ Take Action

Do a Google search of "Hindu gods." How many could you find?

✝ Connect with Jesus

Jesus, help me be brave and courageous in my faith. I want to be strong and not afraid to stand up for You. Forgive me when I don't share with my friends how great You are. Amen.

Around the Word This Week

Each day this week, read a verse and respond to it however you want. Think about it. Write it down on an index card that you can carry with you. Journal about it. Share it with a friend. Pray that the verse will impact you and you will obey it. It's your choice. To get you started thinking about how the Scripture relates to your life, consider the question that follows it.

★ DAY 2

"Be on guard. Stand firm in the faith. Be courageous. Be strong. And do everything with love."   1 Corinthians 16:13-14

Who is the most courageous person you know? Why?

★ DAY 3

*"David continued, 'Be strong and courageous, and do the work. Don't be afraid or discouraged, for the L*ORD *God, my God, is with you. He will not fail you or forsake you. He will see to it that all the work related to the Temple of the L*ORD *is finished correctly.'"*   1 Chronicles 28:20

When have you been afraid? What happened?

 # DAY 4

"Be strong and courageous, all you who put your hope in the LORD!" Psalm 31:24

What do you think it means to put your hope in God?

★ DAY 5

"Be strong and courageous, for you are the one who will lead these people to possess all the land I swore to their ancestors I would give them. Be strong and very courageous. Be careful to obey all the instructions Moses gave you. Do not deviate from them, turning either to the right or to the left. Then you will be successful in everything you do." Joshua 1:6-7

According to this verse, how can you find success in everything?

Over the Weekend

"The wicked run away when no one is chasing them, but the godly are as bold as lions." Proverbs 28:1

How are lions bold? When have you been bold? Did God help you?

WEEK FORTY
Love Mercy

 DAY 1

"O people, the Lord has told you what is good, and this is what he requires of you: to do what is right, to love mercy, and to walk humbly with your God." Micah 6:8

SELENA BEGGED HER OLDER sister Sasha to forgive her and give her another chance. "I promise I won't take your lip gloss again! Really!"

Sasha rolled her eyes. "That's not all you've taken from me. You never ask if you can borrow my clothes and then I see you wearing them. That's like stealing. I don't mind lending, but you have to ask, okay?"

"Okay," Selena said.

But the following week, Selena couldn't resist wearing Sasha's black flip-flops to school. They matched her clothes perfectly! She sneaked them back into Sasha's closet just as Sasha opened the door to her room.

"What are you doing?"

"Nothing."

"What did I tell you? Don't take my stuff without asking!"

Two weeks later, Selena found her favorite hair clip missing, the one with black-and-red ribbon woven through it. "Where is my hair clip?" She rampaged through the house. Finally, she spied it in her younger sister Shelby's hair. She grabbed it and hollered, "That's mine! How dare you take it!"

"I found it on the ground. I'm sorry!" Shelby cried.

"You'll be sorry all right."

Selena had a mercy problem. She wanted everyone else to be merciful to her when she took things, but when her younger sister accidently took her hair clip, she refused to give her mercy.

In today's verse, the Old Testament prophet Micah calls us to love mercy. What does that mean? It means that we learn to be kind and forgiving when others are mean to us or take advantage of us. After all, that's how God is to us. He has mercifully forgiven all our sins, even though we keep sinning. When we freely give mercy to others, we are imitating God. And yes, that means offering forgiveness and mercy to our brothers and sisters!

✎ Take Action

Sometime this week someone will disappoint or hurt you—guaranteed. Right now make the decision to offer that person mercy.

✝ Connect with Jesus

Jesus, I'm not always merciful. I like others to give me mercy, but I'm not a fan of offering it to others. Help me change that, Lord. Make me a person of mercy. Amen.

Around the Word This Week

Each day this week, read a verse and respond to it however you want. Think about it. Write it down on an index card that you can carry with you. Journal about it. Share it with a friend. Pray that the verse will impact you and you will obey it. It's your choice. To get you started thinking about how the Scripture relates to your life, consider the question that follows it.

⭐ DAY 2

"The LORD passed in front of Moses, calling out, 'Yahweh! The LORD! The God of compassion and mercy! I am slow to anger and filled with unfailing love and faithfulness.'"

Exodus 34:6

What does the word *faithfulness* mean? Why do you think God is faithful to us?

★ DAY 3

"God blesses those who are merciful, for they will be shown mercy." Matthew 5:7

Why do you think God shows mercy to those who are merciful?

★ DAY 4

"Once you had no identity as a people; now you are God's people. Once you received no mercy; now you have received God's mercy."   1 Peter 2:10

How have you experienced God's mercy in your life?

★ DAY 5

"There will be no mercy for those who have not shown mercy to others. But if you have been merciful, God will be merciful when he judges you."   James 2:13

According to this verse, why is it important for us to be merciful? What happens when we don't show mercy?

Over the Weekend

"Since God chose you to be the holy people he loves, you must clothe yourselves with tenderhearted mercy, kindness, humility, gentleness, and patience." Colossians 3:12

How does knowing you're loved by God help you to be merciful and kind to others?

 DAY 1

"Even though the fig trees have no blossoms, and there are no grapes on the vines; even though the olive crop fails, and the fields lie empty and barren; even though the flocks die in the fields, and the cattle barns are empty, yet I will rejoice in the Lord! I will be joyful in the God of my salvation! The Sovereign Lord is my strength! He makes me as surefooted as a deer, able to tread upon the heights."   Habakkuk 3:17-19

"WHAT'S THE POINT of following Jesus, anyway?" Jill shot an exasperated look Kamryn's way.

"What do you mean?" Kamryn, Jill's discipleship leader, took a sip of her iced coffee as they chatted at the coffee shop where they met every week.

"So I finally decide to follow Him and all. Then everything falls apart. I don't get it." Jill nibbled a piece of biscotti.

"I'm sorry," Kamryn said. "I know you've been through so much in the past few months."

"You're telling me. My parents splitting up, my sister going off to college, and then my mom announcing that we're moving. It's way too much. It almost feels like God doesn't love me or want me to be happy."

"He does love you."

Jill sighed. "Well, He has a strange way of showing it."

Kamryn opened her Bible to today's verses and read them to Jill. "What this means is that even when things don't go our way, it's still right to praise God."

"That's lame! You mean God wants me to be happy that my parents are divorced?" Jill shook her head.

"No, He grieves over that with you. But He knows that something great happens inside you when you take your eyes off the circumstances around you and choose to think about how awesome God is."

"I don't know. That seems like faking it to me," Jill said.

"This week, I want you to try it. Next time you're sad and upset, turn on one of your worship songs and sing along."

Jill agreed. Throughout the week when things got bad, she sang. And something surprising happened—some of her grief disappeared. From Habakkuk we learn that even when life is hard, we can choose to praise. It's not always easy to learn to praise God when things aren't going our way, but once we get in the habit of doing it, our outlook will change.

✎ Take Action

Do what Jill did when she got upset. Next time life overwhelms you or someone hurts your feelings or school is stressful, turn on an iShine worship song and belt it out. See what happens.

✝ Connect with Jesus

Jesus, the last thing I want to do is praise You when it seems like You're not on the job. Help me to remember how awesome You are when my life is weird or painful. I need to learn to praise You at all times! Amen.

Around the Word This Week

Each day this week, read a verse and respond to it however you want. Think about it. Write it down on an index card that you can carry with you. Journal about it. Share it with a friend. Pray that the verse will impact you and you will obey it. It's your choice. To get you started thinking about how the Scripture relates to your life, consider the question that follows it.

⭐ DAY 2

"Why am I discouraged? Why is my heart so sad? I will put my hope in God! I will praise him again—my Savior and my God!"

Psalm 43:5

What has God done for you that you can praise Him for today?

★ DAY 3

"Always be joyful. Never stop praying. Be thankful in all circumstances, for this is God's will for you who belong to Christ Jesus." 1 Thessalonians 5:16-18

How can someone possibly be joyful all the time? How does that work?

⭐ DAY 4

"Let all that I am praise the LORD; with my whole heart, I will praise his holy name."   Psalm 103:1

What does it mean to praise God from a whole heart? How do we get whole hearts?

★ DAY 5

"Let us offer through Jesus a continual sacrifice of praise to God, proclaiming our allegiance to his name." Hebrews 13:15

Who do you know who praises God all the time? What is his or her life like?

Over the Weekend

"Dear friends, don't be surprised at the fiery trials you are going through, as if something strange were happening to you. Instead, be very glad—for these trials make you partners with Christ in his suffering, so that you will have the wonderful joy of seeing his glory when it is revealed to all the world."

1 Peter 4:12-13

Do you know someone who is going through a trial right now? Write out a prayer for that person.

 DAY 1

*"'Bring all the tithes into the storehouse so there will be
enough food in my Temple. If you do,' says the L*ORD* of
Heaven's Armies, 'I will open the windows of heaven for
you. I will pour out a blessing so great you won't have
enough room to take it in! Try it! Put me to the test!'"*

Malachi 3:10

BLAKE LOVED SAVING MONEY in the bank account his parents
had set up for him. He rarely spent it and regularly checked
to see how much interest his money was earning. Even
though it was pennies, he always felt richer.

One Saturday, Blake went on a mission around the house
to find loose change. He was excited when he came up with
$4.54, after rifling through the couch and chair cushions in

the family room. With this deposit, he would have more than $500 in the bank.

A few weeks later, on their way home from church, Blake's dad asked, "Blake, have you ever considered giving some of your money to the church?"

"Why would I do that?" Blake asked.

"Giving helps us remember that God owns everything. In the Old Testament, the Israelites gave a tithe, about 10 percent of their crops, to the Lord."

Blake knew what 10 percent of his savings meant. Fifty dollars. "I don't know, Dad," he said. "That's a lot of money."

"It's up to you. I'm not going to tell you what to do," his father said. "But I want you to think about this. Do you really believe God will take care of you? Or is it your job to take care of yourself?"

Blake knew the right answer was to trust God for everything, including money, but he also didn't want to part with fifty dollars.

Today's verse comes from the last book of the Old Testament and emphasizes the importance of giving a tithe to God. In the New Testament, believers gave even more than 10 percent. Some sacrificed everything for the sake of Jesus and His followers. They sold homes; they gave their clothing; they collected offerings for poor people in Jerusalem. It's not easy to make those kinds of sacrifices. But there is great joy when we give generously, realizing that our gifts reflect God's abundant blessings to us.

✎ Take Action

Go to WorldVision.org, click on "Ways to Give," and select "Gift Catalog Giving." Find something you'd like to give to a child or family in need and start saving so you can send this gift next Christmas.

✝ Connect with Jesus

Jesus, help me to be a generous person instead of holding on so tightly to my money that I forget that You are the One who provides. Show me someone's need this week so I can meet it. I love You! Amen.

Around the Word This Week

Each day this week, read a verse and respond to it however you want. Think about it. Write it down on an index card that you can carry with you. Journal about it. Share it with a friend. Pray that the verse will impact you and you will obey it. It's your choice. To get you started thinking about how the Scripture relates to your life, consider the question that follows it.

⭐ DAY 2

"If someone has enough money to live well and sees a brother or sister in need but shows no compassion—how can God's love be in that person?"   1 John 3:17

Have you ever needed money or food? If so, how did God provide?

⭐ DAY 3

"No one can serve two masters. For you will hate one and love the other; you will be devoted to one and despise the other. You cannot serve both God and money." Matthew 6:24

Why do you think it's impossible to love money and serve God at the same time?

★ DAY 4

"The trustworthy person will get a rich reward, but a person who wants quick riches will get into trouble."

Proverbs 28:20

Why do people who want quick riches get into trouble? What do they do that gets them in trouble?

★ DAY 5

"Wherever your treasure is, there the desires of your heart will also be." Matthew 6:21

What does it mean to treasure the things God treasures? What does He think is important?

Over the Weekend

"The wicked borrow and never repay, but the godly are generous givers."   Psalm 37:21

Who is the most generous person you know? What makes that person generous?

WEEK FORTY-THREE
Go

 DAY 1

*"Jesus came and told his disciples, 'I have been given all
authority in heaven and on earth. Therefore, go and make
disciples of all the nations, baptizing them in the name of
the Father and the Son and the Holy Spirit. Teach these new
disciples to obey all the commands I have given you. And
be sure of this: I am with you always, even to the end of
the age.'"* Matthew 28:18-20

"IT'S NOT FAIR THAT you're going to Ghana and I have to stay
here," Sahara said.

"I wish you could come." Kimberly opened pictures stored
on her computer. "We'll be in this village. Aren't the kids cute?"

Sahara frowned. "My parents won't let me go on mission

trips, at least not ones overseas. All I ever wanted to do was to go. And now I can't."

Kimberly's big sister, Alice, sat beside them at the breakfast table. "You know, Sahara, it doesn't matter where you are. Or where you go. You're a missionary right now!"

"What? I thought missionaries had to go to Africa or India," Sahara said.

"No," Alice said. "Jesus told His disciples to go into the whole world, which includes our little town. It's all a matter of perspective. You can share Him here, right?"

Sahara smiled a little. "I never thought about it that way. I guess so."

Kimberly closed her laptop. "Yeah, like what about Rachel?"

"What about her?" Sahara remembered their friend Rachel who struggled in school and often went to the counselor's office to cry.

"Praying for her and loving her is being a missionary. So while I'm in Ghana, you can stay home and love Rachel and tell her about Jesus."

As they talked, Sahara learned something important about Jesus' command to go to all the world. The whole world includes her backyard. A missionary is just a Jesus-follower who stays aware of the needs around her and seeks to share Jesus with the people He puts in her life. Some of us may go around the world to share Him. Others may stay home and become missionaries in their schools, to people around them. All of us are responsible for making Jesus known, wherever we are.

✎ Take Action

Find out about your church's missions program and consider becoming a pen pal with someone who is serving Jesus in another part of the world. Or go to www.igoglobal.org. Explore where you would like to go someday. Write it down, pray about it, and see what God will do. (But don't forget to make the most of every opportunity where you live now.)

✝ Connect with Jesus

Jesus, I know You said we are supposed to go and make disciples. Sometimes I forget that it doesn't mean I have to go far away. You want me to go to my school, my family, and my friends and tell them all about You. Forgive me when I'm quiet. Help me be bold and strong and unafraid. Amen.

Around the Word This Week

Each day this week, read a verse and respond to it however you want. Think about it. Write it down on an index card that you can carry with you. Journal about it. Share it with a friend. Pray that the verse will impact you and you will obey it. It's your choice. To get you started thinking about how the Scripture relates to your life, consider the question that follows it.

★ DAY 2

"You will receive power when the Holy Spirit comes upon you. And you will be my witnesses, telling people about me everywhere—in Jerusalem, throughout Judea, in Samaria, and to the ends of the earth."   Acts 1:8

What has Jesus done in your life that you could share with someone? Who do you want to share that with this week? This month?

⭐ DAY 3

"These were his instructions to them: 'The harvest is great, but the workers are few. So pray to the Lord who is in charge of the harvest; ask him to send more workers into his fields.'"

Luke 10:2

Why do you think Jesus asks us to be His workers, to tell others about Him?

⭐ DAY 4

"Again he said, 'Peace be with you. As the Father has sent me, so I am sending you.'" John 20:21

Why does having peace help you want to tell others about Jesus?

⭐ DAY 5

"How will anyone go and tell them without being sent? That is why the Scriptures say, 'How beautiful are the feet of messengers who bring good news!'"   Romans 10:15

What is the good news of the gospel? What did Jesus do for us?

Over the Weekend

"So we are Christ's ambassadors; God is making his appeal through us. We speak for Christ when we plead, 'Come back to God!'"   2 Corinthians 5:20

What does an ambassador do? If you don't know, Google it. What should an ambassador for Jesus do?

 DAY 1

"When you are praying, first forgive anyone you are holding a grudge against, so that your Father in heaven will forgive your sins, too." Mark 11:25

MERRY COULDN'T UNDERSTAND why her best friend Chantal no longer spoke to her. Something must've happened, but it wasn't until the next day at school that she found out what. Chantal told Missy that she didn't want to hang out with Merry anymore because Merry was too smart and made her feel dumb.

Merry found Chantal in the lunchroom and sat beside her. "Hey, I heard what you told Missy," she said.

"So?" Chantal took a bite of her sandwich.

"So, I'm not that smart. Besides, why is it a big deal?"

Chantal looked at her and said sharply, "You got an A on the health test. And then you gloated about it."

Merry left her lunch untouched. "I'm sorry. I was just so happy. I had studied so hard and it was my first A in health."

Chantal grabbed her lunch bag and walked away, leaving Merry even more confused.

For the next few months Chantal ignored Merry. Every time Merry saw her, she kept apologizing. But then Merry got mad. Eventually, her heart grew bitter toward Chantal. It got so bad she couldn't even pray anymore because every time she was quiet enough to pray, she could hear Chantal's accusations.

Even though it doesn't seem fair, if Merry wants to be free from her bitterness, she'll have to forgive Chantal. Forgiving her won't mean that they'll automatically be friends again, but it will help keep Merry's heart from growing cold toward God or other friends. Bitterness and unforgiveness have a way of eating us up on the inside. We only damage ourselves when we hang on to them.

Perhaps the best way to think about forgiveness is to imagine a simple picture. Think of how high a pile your sins would make, stacked up. It's a pretty big mountain, isn't it? Then think about the little offense between you and the person you're trying to forgive. It's barely noticeable. Jesus forgave your mountain. Surely you can trust Him to help you forgive that tiny pile.

✎ Take Action

Think of someone you've been bitter toward. Write that person a letter apologizing for your bad attitude and offering forgiveness for whatever provoked it. Pray about whether you should send the letter or keep it. Often when we write things out, it helps us to forgive.

✝ Connect with Jesus

Jesus, thank You for forgiving me my mountain of sins. I want to be someone who forgives, but it's so hard. The trouble is, I don't want my friends to get away with their sin—I kind of like being mad! Help me let go of my bitterness. Amen.

Around the Word This Week

Each day this week, read a verse and respond to it however you want. Think about it. Write it down on an index card that you can carry with you. Journal about it. Share it with a friend. Pray that the verse will impact you and you will obey it. It's your choice. To get you started thinking about how the Scripture relates to your life, consider the question that follows it.

★ DAY 2

"If you forgive those who sin against you, your heavenly Father will forgive you. But if you refuse to forgive others, your Father will not forgive your sins." Matthew 6:14-15

Why is it so important to forgive people?

⭐ DAY 3

"Peter came to him and asked, 'Lord, how often should I forgive someone who sins against me? Seven times?' 'No, not seven times,' Jesus replied, 'but seventy times seven!'"

Matthew 18:21-22

Do the math. What's 70 x 7? Has anyone ever hurt you that many times?

★ DAY 4

*"I tell you, her sins—and they are many—have been forgiven,
so she has shown me much love. But a person who is
forgiven little shows only little love."*   Luke 7:47

Why is someone who is forgiven much so thankful? Why do
you think that person wants to show more love?

★ DAY 5

"Forgive us our sins, as we forgive those who sin against us. And don't let us yield to temptation."   Luke 11:4

Spend some time writing out your sins and asking God for His forgiveness.

Over the Weekend

"Now that their father was dead, Joseph's brothers became fearful. 'Now Joseph will show his anger and pay us back for all the wrong we did to him,' they said. So they sent this message to Joseph: 'Before your father died, he instructed us to say to you: "Please forgive your brothers for the great wrong they did to you—for their sin in treating you so cruelly." So we, the servants of the God of your father, beg you to forgive our sin.' When Joseph received the message, he broke down and wept."

Genesis 50:15-17

Joseph's brothers sold him into slavery, yet they asked him to forgive them. Why is it hard to forgive members of your own family?

WEEK FORTY-FIVE
Impossible

 DAY 1

"Nothing is impossible with God."   Luke 1:37

"I DON'T THINK GRANDDAD will ever become a Christian," Seth told his mom.

"It's hard, I know." She poured him a glass of milk, then handed him the chocolate syrup. "I've been praying for him ever since I became a Christian."

"That's a long time." Seth stirred the chocolate into the milk.

"I agree. He doesn't seem to want to know God. He's pushed Him away his whole life."

Seth took a bite of a cookie. "So does it really matter if we pray for him? If it's impossible, why even do it?"

His mom got up to put the milk away, then sat next to

353

Seth at the table. "I didn't say it was impossible. With God, nothing is impossible. So we keep praying and hoping and trusting."

"I don't want Granddad to die and not know Jesus."

Seth's mom put her hand on his shoulder. "Neither do I."

All of us have difficult people or situations in our lives. When it seems like we are waiting forever for an answer to our prayers, we can get discouraged and want to quit hoping and praying. Today's verse reminds us that God is bigger than people. He's bigger than circumstances. He's bigger than our perception of our situation. He is that big.

That's what faith is all about, trusting God to do what we cannot. So don't despair. Don't give up believing. Keep praying and trusting that God is big enough to do huge, impossible things.

It's something He specializes in!

✎ Take Action

Think of one thing you believe would be impossible (a relative accepting Jesus, financial help, a relationship restored) and write it down on an index card. Slip it into your Bible. Every time you see the card, pray for God to do the impossible.

✝ Connect with Jesus

Jesus, help me not to give up when situations seem impossible. I want to believe You are big enough to do impossible things. Increase my faith. And please answer my prayer according to Your plan. Amen.

Around the Word This Week

Each day this week, read a verse and respond to it however you want. Think about it. Write it down on an index card that you can carry with you. Journal about it. Share it with a friend. Pray that the verse will impact you and you will obey it. It's your choice. To get you started thinking about how the Scripture relates to your life, consider the question that follows it.

 DAY 2

"Jesus looked at them intently and said, 'Humanly speaking, it is impossible. But not with God. Everything is possible with God.'"   Mark 10:27

What wild, crazy, amazing thing can you trust God for this year?

⭐ DAY 3

"It is impossible to please God without faith."   Hebrews 11:6

Why do you think it's impossible to please God if you don't have faith?

⭐ DAY 4

"'You don't have enough faith,' Jesus told them. 'I tell you the truth, if you had faith even as small as a mustard seed, you could say to this mountain, "Move from here to there," and it would move. Nothing would be impossible.'"

Matthew 17:20

Look back over the past year. How has your faith grown?

⭐ DAY 5

"This is what the LORD of Heaven's Armies says: All this may seem impossible to you now, a small remnant of God's people. But is it impossible for me? says the LORD of Heaven's Armies."

Zechariah 8:6

How does knowing God is Lord over heaven's armies help you trust Him?

Over the Weekend

"Oh, how great are God's riches and wisdom and knowledge! How impossible it is for us to understand his decisions and his ways!" Romans 11:33

Why is it hard to understand God's ways?

DAY 1

"Do to others as you would like them to do to you."

Luke 6:31

JERICHA INVITED WINNIE, her friend from another state who was visiting for the weekend, to hang out with her and her friends at the mall. When they arrived, Jericha didn't introduce Winnie to her friends, which made Winnie feel uncomfortable.

Though they shopped at all of her favorite stores, Winnie wanted to leave because Jericha ignored her, only chatting with her other friends the entire time.

When the girls sat down in the food court for lunch, one of Jericha's friends said, "I'm so sorry. I didn't ask your name. My name is Katy. What is yours?"

"Winnie." Winnie began eating one of her spring rolls.

"That's an awesome name. I've never heard it before." Katy noticed what Winnie had ordered for lunch. "Are those any good?"

"I like them," Winnie said with a smile. "Would you like to try one?" Winnie shared her lunch with Katy, and soon the two were laughing and talking like old friends.

Which of the two girls followed the Golden Rule (see the verse above) in today's story—Jericha or Katy?

If you said Katy, you're right. She remembered what it was like to feel left out—the last time she hung out with her older cousin at the mall, not a soul talked to her. She considered how Winnie must have felt with a bunch of strangers, chattering about people and things she didn't know anything about.

Being able to do what you'd like done to you means slipping on someone else's shoes and seeing life from a different perspective. It means stopping for a moment and asking yourself: *Have I become less selfish over the last year? Am I better at putting others first?*

By nature, all of us are selfish. We see things from our perspective. But Jesus commands us to love others the way we desire to be loved. That means thinking of others when we'd rather think about ourselves. It means meeting someone else's need before we try to get our own needs met.

✎ Take Action

Draw a pair of glasses and write today's Scripture on the lenses. Ask God to help you see someone who has a need that you can help meet.

✝ Connect with Jesus

Jesus, help me to think of others and how they would like to be loved this week. I admit sometimes I'm a Me Monster, thinking only of what I need and want. Help me to turn that around and find ways to take care of others. Amen.

Around the Word This Week

Each day this week, read a verse and respond to it however you want. Think about it. Write it down on an index card that you can carry with you. Journal about it. Share it with a friend. Pray that the verse will impact you and you will obey it. It's your choice. To get you started thinking about how the Scripture relates to your life, consider the question that follows it.

⭐ DAY 2

"Don't just pretend to love others. Really love them. Hate what is wrong. Hold tightly to what is good. Love each other with genuine affection, and take delight in honoring each other."

Romans 12:9-10

Who has loved you with genuine affection and delight?

⭐ DAY 3

"My dear brothers and sisters, how can you claim to have faith in our glorious Lord Jesus Christ if you favor some people over others?" James 2:1

What's wrong with favoring some people over others?

★ DAY 4

"Yes indeed, it is good when you obey the royal law as found in the Scriptures: 'Love your neighbor as yourself.' But if you favor some people over others, you are committing a sin. You are guilty of breaking the law." James 2:8-9

What does it mean to love your neighbor (friend, relative, brother, sister) as yourself?

★ DAY 5

"Live in harmony with each other. Don't be too proud to enjoy the company of ordinary people. And don't think you know it all!" Romans 12:16

Have you ever met a know-it-all? Or someone who wouldn't associate with people he or she didn't approve of? Why does this behavior make God sad?

Over the Weekend

"Don't let evil conquer you, but conquer evil by doing good."

Romans 12:21

What movie have you seen that shows good conquering evil? What were some traits of the hero or heroine?

WEEK FORTY-SEVEN
Assurance

 DAY 1

"I tell you the truth, those who listen to my message and believe in God who sent me have eternal life. They will never be condemned for their sins, but they have already passed from death into life." John 5:24

WHEN DYLAN SPIED HIS favorite candy bar at the store checkout, he wanted it. But he didn't have any money with him, and he doubted his mom would let him have it. Instead of asking his mom, he quickly slipped it into his pocket. As Dylan and his mom were about to walk out of the store, a security officer stopped them. He pointed to Dylan. "May I see what's in your pocket?"

Dylan felt his face turn red, and he saw the look of alarm in his mom's eyes. Slowly, he pulled out the candy. "I took it," he said.

The security guard escorted Dylan to the manager's office. The manager reprimanded Dylan, and Dylan apologized several times for what he did, promising never to steal anything again. After his mom paid for the candy bar, Dylan was let go with a warning.

Later that night, Dylan told his father about what he'd done. He was still shaken by the incident. "Dad, I'm going to hell, aren't I?"

"What do you mean?" his dad asked.

"I broke a commandment, so I'm going to hell."

Dylan's dad put an arm around his son. "We all do stupid things, Dylan. I know I did when I was growing up. And sometimes I still do, even now. The question isn't whether you stole something—you did. The question is, do you still love Jesus and are you sorry for what you did?"

"More sorry than you know," Dylan replied.

"Being a Christ-follower doesn't mean you'll be perfect. What it means is that you're willing to admit when you're wrong. It means being broken and dependent on Jesus. That's what salvation is all about. It's not tied to your obedience."

Dylan let out a long sigh. "You mean I'm still a Christian?"

"From what I can see, yes. But only you know in your heart if you love Jesus."

When we do something wrong, sometimes we question

our salvation, like Dylan did. But God promises that we have *assurance*, a long word that simply means we can rest in knowing what God says is true. Once you give your life to Jesus, your eternity is secure because it is based on what Jesus did on the cross, not on what you do or don't do every day.

✏ Take Action

This week's verses are extremely important for you to know. Choose the one that stands out to you the most, then jot it down on an index card. Memorize the verse.

✝ Connect with Jesus

Jesus, thank You that even when I mess up, You still love me and have assured me that I'll be okay forever. I am grateful for that gift. When I do something wrong, help me to be broken about my sin, confess it, and then rely on You to guide me day by day. Amen.

Around the Word This Week

Each day this week, read a verse and respond to it however you want. Think about it. Write it down on an index card that you can carry with you. Journal about it. Share it with a friend. Pray that the verse will impact you and you will obey it. It's your choice. To get you started thinking about how the Scripture relates to your life, consider the question that follows it.

★ DAY 2

"If you confess with your mouth that Jesus is Lord and believe in your heart that God raised him from the dead, you will be saved. For it is by believing in your heart that you are made right with God, and it is by confessing with your mouth that you are saved." Romans 10:9-10

What do you need to do in order to be saved?

⭐ DAY 3

"Anyone who believes in God's Son has eternal life. Anyone who doesn't obey the Son will never experience eternal life but remains under God's angry judgment."   John 3:36

What does it mean to have eternal life?

★ DAY 4

"He is the one all the prophets testified about, saying that everyone who believes in him will have their sins forgiven through his name." Acts 10:43

Old Testament prophets predicted that Jesus would be born, live on earth, and eventually die on a cross. Does that make it easier to believe in Him today?

 # DAY 5

"There is no condemnation for those who belong to Christ Jesus. And because you belong to him, the power of the life-giving Spirit has freed you from the power of sin that leads to death."

Romans 8:1-2

According to this verse, who frees you from sin's power?

Over the Weekend

"God saved you by his grace when you believed. And you can't take credit for this; it is a gift from God. Salvation is not a reward for the good things we have done, so none of us can boast about it. For we are God's masterpiece. He has created us anew in Christ Jesus, so we can do the good things he planned for us long ago." Ephesians 2:8-10

Does doing a bunch of good stuff get you saved? What saves you?

WEEK FORTY-EIGHT
People-Pleasing

 DAY 1

"Obviously, I'm not trying to win the approval of people, but of God. If pleasing people were my goal, I would not be Christ's servant." Galatians 1:10

"I'M SO TIRED OF VOLLEYBALL," Anna told her sister, Shayna, in the bathroom they shared at home.

"Then don't do it anymore." Shayna finished braiding Anna's hair so it wouldn't be in her face during tournament play that day.

"I can't quit."

"Why not? I mean, it's not good to quit, but in this case, if you don't like it anymore, it could be the right choice." Shayna put her hands on Anna's shoulders. "Can you see yourself as a professional volleyball player?"

377

"I doubt it," Anna said.

"Do you love the game, and are you still having fun?"

"I'm only doing it because Stephanie wants me to. And the coach says she needs me too."

Shayna smiled. "What do you want to do? What does God want you to do?"

Anna made a face. "Quit asking so many questions. I shouldn't have even told you I was tired of volleyball."

Like Anna, sometimes we do things because others want us to. While that's not always a bad thing (nor is it wrong to stick to your commitments), it's important to recognize when we're doing things just so people will like us.

We can also get so caught up in what other people think about us, or whether so-and-so likes us, that we spend a ton of energy working to please them. Today's verse, written by the apostle Paul, emphasizes the importance of shifting our focus from trying really hard to please people to placing our worries about what people think about us on Jesus' shoulders. A way to do that is to ask ourselves a simple question: What would make Jesus smile today?

Pleasing people can make you crazy because it's impossible to impress everyone all the time. But living your life for Jesus and His reputation, instead of your own, will bring you peace.

✎ Take Action

Ask your parents or grandparents if they have ever struggled with trying to please everyone. What happened? What helped them change?

✟ Connect with Jesus

Jesus, sometimes I worry a lot about what people think. I'm sorry. Help me to worry more about what You think and what You want for my life. I would rather have Your approval! Amen.

Around the Word This Week

Each day this week, read a verse and respond to it however you want. Think about it. Write it down on an index card that you can carry with you. Journal about it. Share it with a friend. Pray that the verse will impact you and you will obey it. It's your choice. To get you started thinking about how the Scripture relates to your life, consider the question that follows it.

⭐ DAY 2

"Work willingly at whatever you do, as though you were working for the Lord rather than for people."

Colossians 3:23

Have you ever cleaned your room joyfully? If you never have or it's been a while, do it this week.

 # DAY 3

"For we speak as messengers approved by God to be entrusted with the Good News. Our purpose is to please God, not people. He alone examines the motives of our hearts."

1 Thessalonians 2:4

What does it mean to be a people-pleaser? How can that behavior get you in trouble?

⭐ DAY 4

"Peter and the apostles replied, 'We must obey God rather than any human authority.'"   Acts 5:29

Think of a time where you had to obey God and not listen to someone else's advice. What happened?

⭐ DAY 5

"'Teacher,' they said, 'we know how honest you are. You are impartial and don't play favorites. You teach the way of God truthfully.'" Mark 12:14

Why does playing favorites hurt people?

Over the Weekend

*"Fearing people is a dangerous trap, but trusting the L*ORD
means safety."   Proverbs 29:25

How can fearing people be a trap?

WEEK FORTY-NINE
Online Sin

 DAY 1

"God's will is for you to be holy, so stay away from all sexual sin."

1 Thessalonians 4:3

TEAL STARED AT HIS computer screen. He had been doing research on the Internet for a school paper, and the moment he clicked on what looked like a promising link, he knew he had made a mistake. He had stumbled upon an adult site, yet his curiosity kept him clicking from page to page. Naked men and women filled the screen. As much as he wanted to, Teal couldn't stop looking.

Just then, Teal's father came into his room. Panicked, Teal minimized the page, but he knew by the look on his dad's face that he was busted.

"Son, what are you looking at?" He sat next to Teal.

Teal couldn't talk. He didn't know what to say.

"I'm sad that you've been looking at that stuff and I know you're ashamed."

Teal nodded, then asked, "How . . . ?"

"Because I struggled with this in the past too."

That got Teal's attention. "You did?"

"Yes, I'm very sorry to say it's true. I've learned to turn away from it, but it took a lot of prayer and admitting it to some good friends."

"That must have been embarrassing," Teal said softly.

His dad shook his head regretfully. "It was."

"I'm sorry for looking at that stuff, Dad."

"I know." His dad put his arm around Teal. "But you have to realize that not only is that stuff addictive, it's also sin. It makes you think about things you shouldn't think about. Sexual sin isn't just what you do. It's what you see, what you think about."

Teal's dad is right. That's why Jesus equated looking at someone with lust as the same thing as committing adultery. Sexual sin starts in your mind and heart. What you put in your mind and heart will determine how you act as you get older. Awful images of pornography will mess with the proper, biblical view of sex, and its addictive nature will imprison you. You'll need to see more and more of it, and your addiction will grow into something you can no longer control. Not only that, you'll have to live with more and more shame.

The simple truth is this: Don't dabble. Don't even peek at pornography or raunchy books, even if others try and persuade you. Run away. You'll save yourself a lifetime of pain.

✏️ Take Action

Ask your parents to go to InternetSafety.com/safe-eyes -parental-control-software-b.php and install the Safe Eyes program. This software filter prevents you from being able to click on objectionable sites. Also, be brave enough to have an open phone policy with your parents, where they can see your texts and pictures at any time.

✝ Connect with Jesus

Jesus, I'm young and this kind of stuff creeps me out, but I will say this: I want to be pure. Help me to keep my eyes away from things that You wouldn't want me to watch. Help me be pure. Amen.

Around the Word This Week

Each day this week, read a verse and respond to it however you want. Think about it. Write it down on an index card that you can carry with you. Journal about it. Share it with a friend. Pray that the verse will impact you and you will obey it. It's your choice. To get you started thinking about how the Scripture relates to your life, consider the question that follows it.

★ DAY 2

"Run from sexual sin! No other sin so clearly affects the body as this one does. For sexual immorality is a sin against your own body. Don't you realize that your body is the temple of the Holy Spirit, who lives in you and was given to you by God? You do not belong to yourself, for God bought you with a high price. So you must honor God with your body."

1 Corinthians 6:18-20

What does the apostle Paul say we should do when it comes to sexual immorality?

★ DAY 3

*"Put to death the sinful, earthly things lurking within you.
Have nothing to do with sexual immorality, impurity, lust,
and evil desires. Don't be greedy, for a greedy person is an
idolater, worshiping the things of this world. Because of
these sins, the anger of God is coming. You used to do these
things when your life was still part of this world."*

Colossians 3:5-7

How should our lives be different from the lives of those who
aren't Christians?

⭐ DAY 4

"You say, 'Food was made for the stomach, and the stomach for food.' (This is true, though someday God will do away with both of them.) But you can't say that our bodies were made for sexual immorality. They were made for the Lord, and the Lord cares about our bodies."   1 Corinthians 6:13

Why do you think God is concerned about what we do with our bodies? Our minds?

⭐ DAY 5

"It is what comes from inside that defiles you. For from within, out of a person's heart, come evil thoughts, sexual immorality, theft, murder, adultery, greed, wickedness, deceit, lustful desires, envy, slander, pride, and foolishness. All these vile things come from within; they are what defile you."

Mark 7:20-23

How can people be set free from the list of sins mentioned in these verses?

Over the Weekend

"Run from anything that stimulates youthful lusts. Instead, pursue righteous living, faithfulness, love, and peace. Enjoy the companionship of those who call on the Lord with pure hearts."   2 Timothy 2:22

Why is hanging out with people who share your faith and values helpful?

 DAY 1

"You intended to harm me, but God intended it all for good. He brought me to this position so I could save the lives of many people." Genesis 50:20

LILA COULDN'T FIGURE out why in the world she had to move to another state. Sure, her dad got a job and all, but it would mean she had to leave in the middle of the school year. Her best friend was going to check with her parents to see if Lila could stay with them and finish school. Lila felt so upset that she even told her mom that she refused to move. But neither of her parents would budge on the decision.

The first day of school in the new city, Lila nearly vomited from stress and fear. She hated being a new girl and hated that kids pointed and whispered because she didn't know

393

where things were. Lila deeply missed all her friends and dreaded starting over at a new church and youth group.

But at the end of that first day, she realized that she had prayed more that day than she ever had before in one day. In fact, it felt like she had prayed nonstop. When she came home, she put her backpack in her room and went out to the kitchen. Her mom poured her some milk and set a plate of homemade cookies in front of her. "For your bravery," her mom said.

"I'm not brave," Lila said. "I was afraid the whole day."

"I moved a lot when I was a kid, so I get it," her mom said. "And I'm sorry you had to go through it too."

"Why did we have to move again?"

"We had to or your dad wouldn't have a job right now. I'm praying that things will get better for you soon."

Just as Lila experienced, sometimes God places us in situations we don't like or want. In that moment, it's hard for us to see what God is doing. Think about when you have grown the most in your relationship with Jesus. Was it when things were easy or when things were hard? Today's verse from Genesis is what Joseph said to his brothers after he had revealed his identity to them. He had suffered slavery and wrongful imprisonment because of their actions decades before. Joseph could have yelled at his siblings, harmed them, or turned his back on them, but instead he forgave and trusted that God allowed those hard circumstances to happen for a reason.

Most people grow through difficult circumstances. Joseph's faith-filled words promise us that God is able to do amazing things even when others mean to harm us. In short, He brings good from bad and asks us to trust Him.

✎ Take Action

On a piece of paper, write about the time in your life when you grew the most with Jesus. What happened? How did God bring good from the bad? Put your story away so that the next time you go through something hard, you can pull it out and remember how good God is.

✝ Connect with Jesus

Jesus, sometimes it's hard to believe that You can bring good from bad. Help me have more faith to believe that. I'm tired of my circumstances right now and I need to know You're there. Please show me this week that You are working behind the scenes to bring good from bad. Amen.

Around the Word This Week

Each day this week, read a verse and respond to it however you want. Think about it. Write it down on an index card that you can carry with you. Journal about it. Share it with a friend. Pray that the verse will impact you and you will obey it. It's your choice. To get you started thinking about how the Scripture relates to your life, consider the question that follows it.

★ DAY 2

"God causes everything to work together for the good of those who love God and are called according to his purpose for them." Romans 8:28

How has God caused something good to come from a difficult situation in your life?

⭐ DAY 3

"Whatever is good and perfect comes down to us from God our Father, who created all the lights in the heavens."

James 1:17

What good and perfect gift has God given you this year?

★ DAY 4

"'For I know the plans I have for you,' says the Lord. 'They are plans for good and not for disaster, to give you a future and a hope.'" Jeremiah 29:11

Does knowing that God has plans for you help you today? In what way?

DAY 5

"Because we are united with Christ, we have received an inheritance from God, for he chose us in advance, and he makes everything work out according to his plan."

Ephesians 1:11

What do you think is "an inheritance from God"?

Over the Weekend

"This has been decreed by the messengers; it is commanded by the holy ones, so that everyone may know that the Most High rules over the kingdoms of the world. He gives them to anyone he chooses—even to the lowliest of people."

Daniel 4:17

How, exactly, does God rule over the kingdoms of the world?

WEEK FIFTY-ONE
Practice Sinning

 DAY 1

"We know that God's children do not make a practice of sinning, for God's Son holds them securely, and the evil one cannot touch them." 1 John 5:18

ARWEN HATED THAT SHE LIED. But she'd lied so much growing up, the habit was hard to break. She didn't even say "helpful" lies, the kind that got you out of trouble. No, she said ridiculous lies like, "I had a hamburger for dinner tonight" instead of saying she ate sushi.

When she became a Christian, she hoped all the lying would magically stop. She did lie less, but she couldn't help letting a few slip through. Recently at youth group, her pastor talked about repetitive sinning and shared 1 John 5:18. Arwen's face flushed. She knew it was impossible but she felt he had been reading her phone texts and knew all her secret lies. She slumped in her chair, horrified.

If she were really a Christian, wouldn't this struggle be over? And if she still struggled, what did that mean? That her commitment to Christ was a lie too?

A lot of people struggle with sin, particularly when they keep repeating a specific sin. We do know that Jesus has promised He will make us brand new when we meet Him. So it's painful and stressful when we can't help sinning.

Many of the verses this week help clarify this. Yes, we are made brand spanking new when we meet Jesus, but we still have something called "the flesh," that part of ourselves that wants its own way, all the time. As Christians, it's a daily battle to say no to what the flesh wants and yes to what the Holy Spirit wants.

The cool thing is that the Holy Spirit actually lives inside us! He is available to help us make choices that please Jesus. The other cool thing is that because of Jesus, we can experience forgiveness. Did you know that Jesus died for the sins you committed yesterday as well as today? And although it's hard to wrap your mind around, He also died for the sins you haven't even done yet! That's how powerful His grace is.

Rest there. If you keep sinning in one particular area, remember that sin often gets worse in the dark. If you keep it a secret and never share your struggle, you might end up fighting that sin for years. It's time to be brave—to share your struggle with a close Christian friend and pray together. When you do, the powerful sense of relief you'll feel will confirm that God is listening too.

✎ Take Action

If you're struggling with a particular sin that seems impossible to break free from, be brave enough to share that with a parent, a pastor or youth leader, or a close Christian friend. Pray that God would reveal to you any unconfessed sin in your life.

✝ Connect with Jesus

Jesus, help! I'm struggling with this sin that I can't stop doing. I need You! I need Your perspective. Help me ask the Holy Spirit for help when I'm tempted. And please make me brave (and humble) enough to share my struggle with a friend who is close to You. Amen.

Around the Word This Week

Each day this week, read a verse and respond to it however you want. Think about it. Write it down on an index card that you can carry with you. Journal about it. Share it with a friend. Pray that the verse will impact you and you will obey it. It's your choice. To get you started thinking about how the Scripture relates to your life, consider the question that follows it.

⭐ DAY 2

"Anyone who continues to live in him [Jesus] will not sin. But anyone who keeps on sinning does not know him or understand who he is. Dear children, don't let anyone deceive you about this: When people do what is right, it shows that they are righteous, even as Christ is righteous."

1 John 3:6-7

What do these verses say about the relationship between Jesus and sin? What do you need to do about your relationship with Jesus?

⭐ DAY 3

"I don't really understand myself, for I want to do what is right, but I don't do it. Instead, I do what I hate. But if I know that what I am doing is wrong, this shows that I agree that the law is good. So I am not the one doing wrong; it is sin living in me that does it." Romans 7:15-17

Over the last month, when have you done what is right? When have you done what is wrong? What happened in each instance? How did God help you do what's right? Did you ask for forgiveness when you sinned?

⭐ DAY 4

"We can be sure that we know him if we obey his commandments. If someone claims, 'I know God,' but doesn't obey God's commandments, that person is a liar and is not living in the truth."   1 John 2:3-4

Why does doing what God wants show Him that we love Him?

⭐ DAY 5

"My dear children, I am writing this to you so that you will not sin. But if anyone does sin, we have an advocate who pleads our case before the Father. He is Jesus Christ, the one who is truly righteous. He himself is the sacrifice that atones for our sins—and not only our sins but the sins of all the world."

1 John 2:1-2

According to this verse, how are our sins taken away?

Over the Weekend

"Those who have been born into God's family do not make a practice of sinning, because God's life is in them. So they can't keep on sinning, because they are children of God."

1 John 3:9

Why do you think God calls us His children?

WEEK FIFTY-TWO
Victory

 DAY 1

"I thank you for answering my prayer and giving me victory!"

Psalm 118:21

TIM LOVED PAINTBALL. Once a month, his dad drove Tim and his best friend, Dirk, twenty miles to a paintball field where they could play "war." The three of them usually stayed on the same team. They didn't always win, but afterward they enjoyed talking about what cool things they had done to evade the enemy.

Tim was especially good at camouflaging himself well. He'd stay quiet until an opponent showed himself. Then Tim would emerge from his hiding place and pelt the poor guy.

He loved winning.

In the first round, Tim and Dirk got hit several times, though Tim's dad got a couple of good shots off to score. Still, their team lost. In the second round, Tim worked harder at hiding and scoring, and it paid off! Their team won!

The Christian life is a lot like paintball. Everyone loves victory, but loss is also a part of the game. Whether you win or lose, it's important to keep playing, to keep learning, to keep moving forward.

The difference is that God, through Jesus Christ, has given us the ultimate victory. We may lose many little battles here on earth. We may encounter mean people, difficult situations, disappointment, and pain, but all that will seem small when we walk through eternity and experience the absolute joy and freedom of heaven.

Because Jesus defeated sin and death when He died on the cross, we can look forward to heaven someday if we follow Him. But He also helps us today to have personal victory. We have the power to love people who are hard to love, to give to those in need, to pray for miracles. We can have victory today because the Holy Spirit lives inside us.

Be assured that even when things are hard, Jesus loves us. He died for us. And He is coming again. Those truths are pure victory.

 ## Take Action

Play a game with your family (a board game, a pickup game of basketball—you choose). Who won? How did everyone react?

✝ Connect with Jesus

Jesus, thank You that You have given us victory—victory over sin and death and pain and everything. Thank You that because I believe in You, I'll be with You in heaven someday. Help me to live a victorious life right now. I love You. Amen.

Around the Word This Week

Each day this week, read a verse and respond to it however you want. Think about it. Write it down on an index card that you can carry with you. Journal about it. Share it with a friend. Pray that the verse will impact you and you will obey it. It's your choice. To get you started thinking about how the Scripture relates to your life, consider the question that follows it.

⭐ DAY 2

"The LORD delights in his people; he crowns the humble with victory."   Psalm 149:4

Is it sometimes hard to believe God delights in you? Why or why not?

⭐ DAY 3

"When our dying bodies have been transformed into bodies that will never die, this Scripture will be fulfilled: 'Death is swallowed up in victory. O death, where is your victory? O death, where is your sting?'"   1 Corinthians 15:54-55

How do we gain victory over death?

 **DAY 4**

"In this way, he disarmed the spiritual rulers and authorities. He shamed them publicly by his victory over them on the cross." Colossians 2:15

Why does the Cross mean victory for us?

⭐ DAY 5

"The LORD is my strength and my song; he has given me victory." Psalm 118:14

Recall the last time you won a game or a competition. How did it feel? How does knowing God brings victory help you today?

Over the Weekend

"Thank God! He gives us victory over sin and death through our Lord Jesus Christ."   1 Corinthians 15:57

According to this verse, why should we thank God?

About the Author

MARY DEMUTH is the author of fourteen books, including parenting books and novels for young adults. She's spent several years as a discipleship group leader to teen girls and has a strong heart for preteens and teens. In 2008, she accompanied her then twelve-year-old son to Ghana to watch his dream of bringing water to a village unfold. Prior to that, her family helped plant a church in southern France. Mary and her husband, Patrick, live in Texas with their three teens. Meet Mary at www.marydemuth.com.

Spiritual, life-changing content *by* Christian teens, *for* today's tweens.

iShine is a unique ministry dedicated to helping tweens develop faith that will last a lifetime as they find their value, identity, and purpose in Christ. iShine reaches tweens, families, and churches through resources like

- *iShine KNECT*—the #1 highest-rated Christian tween television program in the world (now in its fourth season!)
- Music videos and CDs, as well as online streaming of Christian and family-friendly hit music
- Live events and festivals: high-energy, biblically-based live performances with uplifting messages, multimedia interactive projection, and state-of-the art effects—performed by today's top teen artists.
- Multimedia Christian preteen curriculum and resources for churches
- iShinelive.com offers daily Bible verses, games, *KNECT* TV episodes on demand, online chat, online prayer forum, and resources for parents and pastors.
- Social media: Find and follow iShine on 🐦 Twitter and 📘 Facebook!
- And much more!

To check out this amazing ministry, visit www.ishinelive.com. CP0587

ATTENTION TWEENS: This Bible was created specifically for you!

ISBN 978-1-4143-4814-8

ISBN 978-1-4143-4815-5

The Bible is God's way of telling us who he is and who we are. The *iShine Bible* is about helping you understand how God looks at you (did you know you're a VIP in God's eyes?) and will help you face the most important decisions of your life. You'll find lots of features just for tweens about real-life issues and questions that you face. Plus, there's a cool section in the front called the "iShine index," so when you think of an issue or question you have, just look there. It'll give you advice and tell you where the Bible talks about that very issue.

So get your hands on the *iShine Bible* and start living like the VIP you really are!

CP0588